'In a concise and masterful way, Iain Quinn has provided a portrait of the celebrated Swiss American musician Rudolph Ganz, as well as an overview of the attempts that Ganz and others made to standardize *The Star-Spangled Banner*. It is an engaging story of history, music, patriotism, and politics'.
   Larry Alan Smith, *Composer and Professor Emeritus and Former Dean, The Hartt School, University of Hartford*

Rudolph Ganz, Patriotism, and Standardization of The Star-Spangled Banner, 1907–1958

This book examines the succession of events toward the potential standardization of the music for 'The Star-Spangled Banner' from an initial letter to President Roosevelt in 1907 to the 1958 congressional hearings on the National Anthem, and the later work of the Swiss-Born American pianist, Rudolph Ganz. These events took place across five decades when a culture of public patriotism was especially pronounced for immigrant musicians. This book contextualizes the complementary experiences of a leading immigrant musician, Ganz, who successfully navigated the world of public patriotism while pursuing the realization of a standardized version. The materials are discussed through the lens of the performance practice.

The legacy of standardization has not previously been examined. The response and actions of an immigrant, Ganz, in a culture of necessary patriotism for foreign-born artists shed important new light on this topic. It demonstrates the challenges, fears, and cultural expectations regarding the standardization of an important patriotic work.

Iain Quinn is Professor of Organ and Coordinator of Sacred Music at Florida State University. He is also the author of *The Development and Genesis of an English Organ Sonata* (2017), *The Organist in Victorian Literature* (2017), and *Music and Religion in the Writings of Ian McEwan* (2023).

Rudolph Ganz, Patriotism, and Standardization of The Star-Spangled Banner, 1907–1958

Iain Quinn

LONDON AND NEW YORK

First published 2024
by Routledge
4 Park Square, Milton Park, Abingdon, Oxon OX14 4RN

and by Routledge
605 Third Avenue, New York, NY 10158

Routledge is an imprint of the Taylor & Francis Group, an informa business

© 2024 Iain Quinn

The right of Iain Quinn to be identified as author of this work has been asserted in accordance with sections 77 and 78 of the Copyright, Designs and Patents Act 1988.

All rights reserved. No part of this book may be reprinted or reproduced or utilised in any form or by any electronic, mechanical, or other means, now known or hereafter invented, including photocopying and recording, or in any information storage or retrieval system, without permission in writing from the publishers.

Trademark notice: Product or corporate names may be trademarks or registered trademarks, and are used only for identification and explanation without intent to infringe.

British Library Cataloguing-in-Publication Data
A catalogue record for this book is available from the British Library

Library of Congress Cataloging-in-Publication Data
Names: Quinn, Iain, 1973– author.
Title: Rudolph Ganz, patriotism, and standardization of the Star-Spangled Banner, 1907-1958 / Iain Quinn.
Description: [1.] | Abingdon, Oxon ; New York : Routledge, 2023. | Includes bibliographical references and index.
Identifiers: LCCN 2023034223 (print) | LCCN 2023034224 (ebook) | ISBN 9781032554181 (hardback) | ISBN 9781032554198 (paperback) | ISBN 9781003430582 (ebook)
Subjects: LCSH: Star-spangled banner (Song) | Ganz, Rudolph, 1877–1972. | Music—Political aspects—United States—History—20th century.
Classification: LCC ML3561.S8 Q55 2023 (print) | LCC ML3561.S8 (ebook) | DDC 782.42/15990973—dc23/eng/20230808
LC record available at https://lccn.loc.gov/2023034223
LC ebook record available at https://lccn.loc.gov/2023034224

ISBN: 978-1-032-55418-1 (hbk)
ISBN: 978-1-032-55419-8 (pbk)
ISBN: 978-1-003-43058-2 (ebk)

DOI: 10.4324/9781003430582

Typeset in Times New Roman
by codeMantra

To Arianne and our family

Contents

	List of figures	xi
	Acknowledgments	xiii
	Permissions	xv
	Introduction	1
1	An Immigrant's Perspective – The Role of Public Patriotism	5
2	The National Anthem and the Challenge of Standardization	36
3	The Advocacy of the Immigrant – Ganz and The Star-Spangled Banner	66
	Bibliography	85
	Index	89

Figures

1.1	Eleanor Roosevelt, 'Music Should Go On! A Message from the First Lady' (1950)	25
2.1	The Star Spangled Banner, pub. Thomas Carr (1814)	40
2.2	The Star-Spangled Banner – Proposed Official Version supported by the National Music Council (1958)	51
2.3	The Star-Spangled Banner, arr. Paul Taubman (ca. 1958)	56
3.1	The Star-Spangled Banner, arr. Rudolph Ganz (ca. 1965)	77

Acknowledgments

I am indebted to many people for their support of this book. The initial idea for writing about Rudolph Ganz and the National Anthem came as the result of two talks I presented in 2018 when I was the Rudolph Ganz Fellow at The Newberry Library. I will be forever grateful to D. Bradford Hunt, Keelin Burke, and Alison Hinderliter for their guidance during this fellowship and for the company of fellows that offered such valuable insights. I also extend my thanks to Julie Bartlett Nelson, Archivist, Calvin Coolidge Presidential Library & Museum, for graciously helping to solve a particular mystery regarding Rudolph Ganz's performance at The White House. I also remain grateful to Lynn Eaton, Savannah Brooke Long, and Mieko Palazzo at the Special Collections Research Center, George Mason University Libraries, who examined the papers of Representative Joel Broyhill. Permissions were sought for all correspondence published in this volume, and I deeply appreciate the kindness and enthusiasm expressed during this process. Alison Hinderliter's graciousness in checking materials nearer to publication was deeply appreciated. Emmy Táncsics' comments on an early draft were invaluable as were the observations of reviewers for which I am grateful.

Rudolph Ganz's papers at The Newberry Library offer a treasure trove of material regarding the first half of the century in American music. His interests were broad, and his retention of documents, which often include handwritten commentaries, is significant. It is possible to see a musician who was a deep thinker about the prospects for American musicmaking in the twentieth century while Europe rebuilt postwar but equally the level of concern that was being felt by many successful immigrant musicians. Above all, Ganz demonstrates the possibilities that were within reach for someone who was willing to navigate this delicate balance while remaining supportive of many colleagues who, in turn, supported him. Although not an advocate for self-promotion, he was certainly an ardent and compelling spokesman for the profession and was relentless in his pursuit of advancing the cause of music to a wider educated audience.

Permissions

Letters from Rudolph Ganz to Edwin Hughes, National Music Council used by permission of The Newberry Library
Letter from Howard Hanson to Rudolph Ganz used by permission of the Howard Hanson Institute for American Music
Letters from Edwin Hughes, National Music Council to Rudolph Ganz used by permission of the National Music Council
Letter from H. W. Heinsheimer, G. Schirmer to Rudolph Ganz used by permission of G. Schirmer, Inc.
Letter from Harold Spivacke, Chief, Music Division, Library of Congress to Rudolph Ganz used by permission of the Library of Congress

Excerpt from Dr. Rudolph Ganz, "The Star-Spangled Banner," *Music Clubs*, April 1965 used by permission of the National Federation of Music Clubs

Reprinting of the cover of *Musical America*, February 10, 1942, including 'A Message from the First Lady' by permission of Musical America.
Reprinting of Rudolph Ganz's version of 'The Star-Spangled Banner' by permission of The Newberry Library.

Introduction

This book examines the succession of events toward the potential standardization of the music for the 'Star-Spangled Banner' from an initial letter to President Theodore Roosevelt in 1907 to the 1958 congressional hearings on The Star-Spangled Banner. These events took place across five decades when a culture of public patriotism was especially pronounced for prominent immigrant musicians. In this study, public patriotism refers to examples of patriotism in a public setting including performances, compositions, and public writings.

This book contextualizes the complementary experiences of a leading immigrant musician, the well-known Swiss-born American pianist, Rudolph Ganz (1877–1972), who successfully navigated the world of public patriotism while pursuing the realization of a standardized version. The central focus of this book in relation to the National Anthem will be the nature of performance practice and a continuing debate during the period of study about whether an accurate musical text could ultimately be achieved or, arguably, should be achieved. As such, the texts are examined from the perspective of a performing musician, noting the challenges that many previous debates, not least the 1958 congressional hearings, have presented. This specific aspect of the legacy of performance in relation to the National Anthem in a critical period of American political history, especially when considering the varying political climate for immigrant musicians, has not previously been analyzed chronologically. Therefore, the approach in this book is to follow a chronological approach in each chapter and more broadly across the book in order to show both advancements in discourse and relative impediments. This also raises the question of whether standardization is now impossible to consider in our own time when congressional discussions are considerably more partisan, and I discussed this in the final section.

The added consideration of the views of a prominent immigrant musician like Ganz provides an additional level of context, especially because many immigrant musicians were conducting or otherwise personally performing the National Anthem. Highly respected across several musical disciplines, Ganz freely asked questions about what might be a suitable path forward and

DOI: 10.4324/9781003430582-1

enlisted the support of key figures to that end, not least the composer and administrator, Howard Hanson. This study not only notes the contributions of Ganz but also asks whether his decision to become involved in this discussion was unavoidable in order to demonstrate his own approach to patriotism. He drew on the concerns of American-born musicians regarding the balance in the programming of American and Western European music while diplomatically navigating his own position as an immigrant musician. His approach was carefully judged *via media*.

Ganz championed the cause of standardization and, ultimately, the work of the 1958 congressional committee hearings, for much of his later career. He had long presented himself as a loyal immigrant while also acknowledging that he felt uncomfortable by the expectation of unabashed patriotism in public forums in American life. Many of Ganz's European colleagues ran afoul of the public, press, and politicians but Ganz exercised a nuanced approach while furthering his agenda. Rather than respond to potential censure, he made bold and often lengthy statements and was tenacious in his approach regarding the National Anthem.

This book begins with a study of his many patriotic statements that reinforced his loyalty to American musicians, institutions, and the unique role that the country could assume after World War II. His later correspondence with prominent figures in the musical world concerning the National Anthem shows the extent to which the questions about the National Anthem first raised at the beginning of the century by Elsie M. Shawe, director of music in the St. Paul Public Schools, in her 1907 letter to President Theodore Roosevelt remained unresolved, despite the consistent agreement among leading national figures that a standardized version of the National Anthem was necessary.

Ganz was a prominent figure in American musical life in the first half of the twentieth century as a performer, composer, educator, and administrator. By contextualizing his writings as an immigrant working within the musical community amid a continuing culture and fear of accusations of subversion, a greater understanding of the debates surrounding the anthem is brought to light. This text follows Ganz's careful assimilation into American society as an immigrant who was often misidentified as German; the historic legacy of the national discussion of a standardized version of the National Anthem; the cultural climate that predated three days of congressional hearings in 1958; and Ganz's subsequent correspondence with senior figures of the music profession following the hearings. In studying this period, my research contextualizes and complements the research of E. Douglas Bomberger, Mark Clague, Annegret Fauser, Marc Ferris, Jessica Geinow-Hecht, Richard Hill, William Lichtenwanger, Oscar Sonneck, and Patrick Warfield.[1]

To this day, there is no official version of either the words or the tune of the 'Star-Spangled Banner'. The large vocal range required to sing the anthem means that it is often sung in public settings by a soloist rather than by all present, and there is little consistency between performances. When Representative Joel T. Broyhill (R-VA) realized this situation after receiving a letter from high school students in 1955 that he couldn't easily answer, he decided to pursue his inquiry formally. Ultimately, this led to three days of hearings in 1958 by a Subcommittee of the Committee of the Judiciary. The discussions in the hearings demonstrate both integrity and self-interest on the part of the expert witnesses in addition to sometimes shocking naivete and political maneuvering by members of Congress. Alternative musical versions are suggested, complaints about performing styles are registered, arguments about the nature of different ensemble requirements are debated, and questions of subversion and foreign influence are raised.

When examined with Ganz's pursuit of a standardized version, a narrative emerges that explains the challenge, and why it remains unsolved, despite the support of leading contemporary figures. These included Howard Hanson, then dean of the Eastman School of Music, who noted that there should be a 'non-eccentric' version[2] of the National Anthem. As an immigrant, Ganz found the lack of a commonly accepted score both bewildering and disrespectful, while also easily solvable. This book shows the contrasting impressions of someone encountering America as an immigrant and the difficult political ramifications of the congressional world that musicians had to navigate. Ganz retained a copy of the published hearings in his records, his letters to colleagues, as well as his own version of the National Anthem as he thought it should be written. In this respect, Ganz's interest as an immigrant in the National Anthem was a distinct fascination, and his correspondence helps to draw a line between the musical and political climates of the time. Ganz was proud to have become an American citizen; he promoted the works of American composers in his own concerts and encouraged students to consider the works of American composers. But the lack of a standardized score for a piece as important as the National Anthem utterly baffled him.

As the hearings demonstrated, even when musical and textual matters are discussed by musicians, the politics of the environment engenders arguments far beyond simple, logical remedies. This book examines how, despite the inconsistencies with music, text, and performing styles, the 'Star-Spangled Banner' remains uniquely associated with individualism that began with its original composition.

After the 1958 hearings, Broyhill persisted in his regular calls for a standardized version including a bill that was presented in 1973 during his final term in office. The evidence was comprehensive and had evolved over sixty-six years, but the timing could not have been worse as Congress was about to be focused on another matter – Watergate.

Notes

1. E. Douglas Bomberger, "Taking the German Muse out of Music: *The Chronicle* and US Musical Opinion in World War I," *Journal of the Society for American Music*, 14/2 (2020); Mark Clague, *O Say Can You Hear?* (New York: W. W. Norton, 2022); Annegret Fauser, *Sounds of War: Music in the United States during World War II* (New York: Oxford University Press, 2013); Marc Ferris, *Star-Spangled Banner* (Baltimore: Johns Hopkins University Press, 2014); Jessica C. E. Gienow-Hecht, *Sound Diplomacy: Music and Emotions in Transatlantic Relations, 1850-1920* (Chicago: University of Chicago Press, 2009); Richard S. Hill, "A Proposed Official Version of the Star Spangled Banner," *Notes*, 15/1 (1957), 33; William Lichtenwanger, "Star-Spangled Bibliography," *College Music Symposium*, 12 (1972), 98; William Lichtenwanger, "Star-Spangled Banner. What Again?," *The Sonneck Society Newsletter*, 12/2 (Summer 1986), 59–51; Oscar George Sonneck and Library of Congress. Music Division. "The Star Spangled Banner" (Revised and Enlarged From the "Report" On the Above And Other Airs, Issued In 1909). (Washington: Govt. print. off., 1914); Patrick Warfield, "Educators in Search of an Anthem: Standardizing 'The Star-Spangled Banner' During the First World War," *Journal of the Society for American Music*, 12/3 (2018), 268–316.
2. Letter from Howard Hanson to Rudolph Ganz, Eastman School of Music. August 3, 1964.

1 An Immigrant's Perspective – The Role of Public Patriotism

Rudolph Ganz was born in Zürich in 1877. He studied the cello with Friedrich Hegar and the piano with Robert Freund and, his great-uncle, Carl Eschmann-Dumer. His composition lessons were with Charles Blanchet and later with Heinrich Urban. He was a student of Ferruccio Busoni in Berlin, and Busoni dedicated his first sonatina to him. Ganz made his Berlin debut in 1899 performing Beethoven's fifth concerto and Chopin's first concerto. In the following year, he conducted the Berlin Philharmonic Orchestra in the first performance of his own *First Symphony*. He then undertook European and American tours including performances in New York and Boston with Felix Weingartner and Wilhelm Gericke. From 1901 to 1905, he was head of the piano department at the Chicago Musical College. Following several years of touring, he became the director of the Chicago Musical College in 1929 and a president five years later. He remained as a member of the faculty and an administrator until 1954. Between 1921 and 1927, he was the music director of the St. Louis Symphony Orchestra, and between 1939 and 1949, he conducted the Young People's Concerts with both the New York Philharmonic Orchestra and the San Francisco Symphony Orchestra. Ganz was a strong advocate for contemporary music and the broadening of musical tastes. In addition to Ravel's dedication of *Scarbo* to him, he was also a noted champion of the works of Bartók, d'Indy, Korngold, Loeffler with American audiences.[1]

In 1925, Ganz became a naturalized US citizen. At this point, he was already well ensconced in American musical life. His debut in the Music Hall of the Fine Arts Building in Chicago had taken place on May 10, 1902; he had performed with the Chicago Symphony Orchestra (1903), New York Philharmonic, and Boston Symphony Orchestra (1906); toured throughout North America (from 1905 onward); taught at the Institute of Musical Arts, New York (1915); established the summer music colony, 'Camp Mary,' in Naples, Maine (1915–1917); been appointed as permanent conductor of the St. Louis Symphony Orchestra (1921); guest conducted the Los Angeles Philharmonic (1923); and recorded for the Victor label with the St. Louis Symphony Orchestra (1924), and he was the dedicatee of Charles Griffes' *The White Peacock* (1915). He was clearly enamored of American life, the forward-thinking mindset, the opportunity to chart a course unimpeded by long traditions, and also in relative awe of some institutions. To illustrate this, I shall discuss several documents that Ganz retained in his papers, now housed at the Newberry Library. Ganz was a savvy diplomatic communicator, and he tailored his remarks to the audience at hand. This extended especially toward his approach to Americans and to America more broadly. Ganz had arrived in America during the interwar years, held prominent positions in the following decades, and understood the power of words to shape opinions. When considering his writings, there is an immediate impression of him seeming in thrall of individuals and institutions and absorbed in the possibility of America being a beacon for artistic progress in the future. These commentaries are laced with a constant tone of patriotism. However, he is not beyond the manipulation of language to reinforce an opinion that demonstrates this patriotism as will be shown when he refers to Damrosch's 'German'[2] counterpoint as subversive and by his strong offense at the Karl Muck scandal.[3] Ganz had been working in the United States since 1902, and during the later period (before his naturalization in 1925), there were considerable challenges for foreign-born musicians following the US declaration of war on April 6, 1917. These had started to develop at the beginning of the war in Europe but were magnified when the United States entered the war. This sequence of events had a particular bearing for Ganz because he was frequently misidentified as German.

Prior to this period, the cultural relationship between Germany and the United States had been especially productive, and between 1815 and 1914, nine thousand American students studied in Germany.[4] The governing body of the New York Philharmonic, founded in 1842, was mostly German and their meetings took place in locations that were well known to the German-American community.[5] In 1911, the German consul in Atlanta noted how the performance of Engelbert Humperdinck's *Die Königskinder* at the Metropolitan Opera had met with great success, presented before an audience of 6,500, and that he had been elected Vice President of the Philharmonic Society in Atlanta with the hope of promoting German music.[6] Writing of the interest that Americans showed in Germany, Jessica Gienow-Hecht comments that 'Americans, like people elsewhere, regarded German music as a universal language, on both the musical as well as the spiritual level' while noting that what remained peculiar to the American perspective was a complete lack of self-confidence vis-à-vis the international music scene; music had to be imported from abroad, preferably from Germany.[7] In 1914, one-fifth of Americans claimed German ancestry.[8]

As E. Douglas Bomberger has observed, from the entry of America into the war up until the Armistice on November 11, 1918, the opposition to German musical influence in American musical life became increasingly pronounced. One objection focused on German repertoire in concert programs with a secondary objection to conductors, soloists, and orchestral players. It was particularly noted how long foreign-born musicians had been in the United States and whether they had begun or completed the naturalization process.[9] After the Muck scandal (discussed later), numerous musicians were obliged to leave their positions, and the Philadelphia Orchestra removed all unnaturalized members.[10] Bomberger's article examines the role of *The Chronicle*, which he describes as a 'shadowy propaganda magazine', as a significant force in the publication of 'fake news' stories that were aimed at the wealthy elite of their subscription base. Published from March 1917 to November 1918, the magazine influenced the banning of German-language operas at the Metropolitan Opera and the 'near-elimination of German repertoire from US orchestral programmes'.[11] In the summer of 1918, the journal included articles on 'Taking the German Muse out of Music' (July), 'Intern all German Music' (August), and 'There is a Danger in German Music' (September). Prominent performers were expected to declare their patriotism publicly or be shamed if they failed to do so.[12] The following extracts from the last article, written by Cleveland Moffett, indicate the strident tone that was enabled and encouraged:

> Let us concede that German music is the finest music in the world—which it is not. Let us admit that Beethoven, Brahms, Wagner, Liszt, Strauss and all the rest of them are the greatest musicians the world has ever known or ever will know—which is an absurdity. All that being granted, I, nevertheless, maintain that we should drive German music out of America; from all homes, churches, theatres, concert halls, opera houses and other places where music is played, sung or produced.
>
> The musicians of Germany speak with the soul of Germany, and out of the soul of Germany came the ravishing of Belgium, the sinking of the Lusitania. German music is beautiful – yes – but it tends to soften our hearts when we must harden them against compromise with evil: it has a sinister potency as German propaganda. There is *danger* to the Allies in German music.
>
> Am I preaching hatred of Germany?
> Yes—for the present!
> Germany wanted this war and prepared for it for years. Germany could have prevented this war even at the last moment, and did not. Why should we not hate Germany?
>
> We must hate the Germans, just as we must use poison gas against them, and bombard their cities with long-distance guns and follow all their hellish methods of war efficiency.
>
> *Hate is a weapon!*[13]
>
> "Lord forgive them not for they know what they are doing!" cries the French poet in the French hymn of hate.
>
> I agree with him.

8 An Immigrant's Perspective – The Role of Public Patriotism

The music critic, W. J. Henderson, had suggested in a 1917 article in the *New York Sun* titled 'Rising Tide of Sentiment against German Music' that the problem with anti-German sentiment stretched back years when German musicians had celebrated the sinking of the *Lusitania*, although he regretted that ultimately these opinions had tainted the reputation of the violinist, Fritz Kreisler. Kreisler had only recently been discharged from the Austrian army, and his performances had latterly been the subject of boycotts and cancellation to such an extent that he stopped performing until the war ended:[14]

> It has been shown in no uncertain manner that this great artist is to suffer in most places for the sins of the propagandists, who have transformed the mildest of music lovers into determined foes of all things Teutonic.[15]

However, criticism did not solely extend to musicians with a Germanic background. In 1917, the American soprano, Geraldine Farrar, was rebuked for remaining seated during a performance of the National Anthem.[16]

As Ganz was assimilating to America during this period and beginning what would be an extensive career in the country, it is unsurprising that he should seek not just to distance himself from colleagues who showed German connections but instead to assert an especially pro-American stance. He had not been in the country that long, and his career could have easily come to an abrupt end if he was labeled as unpatriotic.

Rather than wait to be asked about his patriotism, he instead spoke about it and acted upon it often. As an example of his performances, he participated in a benefit concert for the 69th Regiment fighting in France that was held at the New York City Hippodrome in September 1918. John McCormack, Amelita Galli-Curci, and Carolina Lazzari were also performers.[17] Ultimately, his displays of patriotism would lead to his great interest in the National Anthem and what he saw as the essential need to standardize the music and related performance practice. However, prior to this, he had to ensure that the culture of distrust surrounding musicians that could in any sense be identified (or in his case misidentified) as German stayed far away from him. Instead, he presented himself as the model immigrant, thrilled with the New World, and all that it could offer to him and to the future of music. Ganz excluded music by contemporary German composers from his programs and also resigned from the Society of German Composers even though he was a founding member.[18]

By 1921, Ganz was the dedicatee of more than twenty works by American composers and gave the first performances of John Alden Carpenter's *Krazy Cat* (1921) and Howard Hanson's *Nordic* symphony (1922).[19] In the Ganz papers at the Newberry Library, there is a newspaper cutting titled 'American Composers Here' from the Cincinnati Enquirer (November 25, 1950) with a photo of Ganz alongside Howard Hanson and Quincy Porter and the conductor Thor Johnson.[20] The photo was taken during the intermission of a concert (November 24, 1950) of the Cincinnati Symphony Orchestra, directed by

Johnson, at which the works of Ganz, Hanson, and Porter were performed. The occasion was a performance 'in honor of the National Association of Schools of Music whose national conference was taking place. It encapsulates the nature of Ganz's self-identification as both an American and a musical figure in the company of leading members of the profession. The presence of this cutting among his saved papers further amplifies the importance of this circumstance to him personally.

Ganz continued his promotion of patriotism and American ideals during World War II as doubts about foreign influence resurfaced again. As Annegret Fauser has noted, Americans did not expect the elimination of German music in programs, as they had in the previous war.[21] But in 1938, the House Un-American Activities Committee had been formed to investigate not only foreign-born citizens but also US citizens born on American soil. The potential threat to Ganz, amid another war with Germany, was once again very much present. After 1959, he performed with his second wife, Esther LaBerge, a mezzo soprano, and their programs included the music of Samuel Barber, John Cage, Elliott Carter, Aaron Copland, John La Montaine, and Ned Rorem, and the piano works of Samuel Barber, Paul Bowles, Leon Kirchner, Robert Muczynski, Walter Piston, and Ben Weber.[22]

In establishing Ganz's response to his life as an immigrant, the following document is especially interesting. He discusses a visit to the White House during the period of President Coolidge's administration (1923–1929) with a sense of wonder at the proceedings and his interaction with the President. Ganz was a musician of high standing who was used to being in social settings and meeting important figures. However, he retells this anecdote with the tenor of being awestruck by the entire proceedings, which suggests it was being written for an American audience. He makes it clear how honored he was to attend an event at The White House and how humbled he was by the brief exchange with the president. Despite initially commenting on not being eager to meet him, the positive memory remained a special one. There is a fairytale arc to the narrative beginning with his doubts and ending with the 'land of dreams.'

The Whitehouse [*sic*] [undated]

Not that I was particularly anxious to go there because the President appeared to be Mr. Coolidge. He did not say much anyway and when he spoke it was not to my liking. But after all, to shake hands with the President of the U.S.A., to be his guest, to experience the First Lady's smile at short distance, to play on the famous golden piano which went easily out of tune I had heard and before an audience of distinguished Americans! What excitement, to say the least. Mr. Junge of Steinway and Sons was the guiding hand that always led the artists thru the portals of the President's residence. Appropriately we stayed at the Mayflower.

8 P.M. The short introductions to the taxi driver were "White House, front entrance!" My heart jumped. Front entrance! Shades of Haydn, Mozart appeared before my eyes. I smiled at them: "Did you hear that, <u>front entrance!</u>" And dear old Joseph Haydn, maître de chapelle de la cour de conte Esterhazy, had to come in thru the service door. The portal of the servants, eat his meals with them, then put on his Kapellmeister frock, go to [the] front of the Castle where the highborne [sic] low-brows were waiting for the music to begin. It had taken a long time indeed for this graduation to the front door. We had arrived. Two derby-hatted plainclothes-men looked us over. Our innocent faces shortened the ritual. We were inside, and were greeted by some very official looking gentleman. A charming, handsome naval officer broke the temperature of the surroundings. Smilingly he assured me that I should feel at home since he would act as my escort during the entire evening. He was a most sympathetic human being. He informed me immediately that there would be a little supper after the program [with] the President, Mrs. Coolidge and about 12 of their intimate friends. He was worried about the fact that under the current Republican Administration nothing better than a scant cigar would be offered. As I do not smoke much and cigars only once every 5 years, I remained calm. The absence of liquor at any functions seemed to upset him for my benefit. We waited patiently in a small room until the grand Gala-dinner came to an end. Mr. Junge wanted to be sure that I should be gracious in presenting myself and that I should not be disappointed if the President would greet me after the concert and dismiss the whole affair with the usual 3-word speech, "I thank you". There I was on the improvised stage with the golden piano. I shall never forget the thrilling picture that I was facing: the President, the First Lady, members of the Cabinet, Generals, Admirals, Ambassadors galore, about 250 names in American History. They were attentive and most cordial and I enjoyed offering the best I knew. The final number concluded [and] the President stood up, came towards my nonpolitical platform. I rushed to meet him half way on the floor. He had taken my hand, and looking me in the eye, he smilingly (I even thought affectionately) said in a slow clear voice: "It has been a great pleasure to have you with us tonight". I nearly swooned...I counted them quickly...12 words...4 times as many as the usual ones – what an event – what a distinction...what an avalanche of conversation. Mrs. Coolidge took me out of my stupor. She loved music, she said. And I deeply appreciated every word that followed. Her personal charm was simply disarming. Without much ceremony the President suddenly offered his arm to his wife, turned to his guests, who stood in groups all over the room and announced as loudly and as dryly: "Good night, everybody" and disappeared thru a door. I well noticed the commotion and astonishment caused by this unexpected and unusual departure. Little did I realize that the happiness of this presidential adventure would be punctuated somewhat a few moments later. We had our little supper alright. Some very delightful cultured people made the short gathering most agreeable. Still the shade of Joseph Haydn was hovering

over my mind, and I could not help reminding myself of the fact that the Father of our Country [George Washington] and the Father of the Symphony [Franz Josef Haydn] saw the Light of the World the same year [1732]. (The symphonic shade urged me.) I asked my very friendly escort who else came to this affair thru the front door as Mr. Junge and I did. The answer was staggering. "No one else." The guests always enter by the West door.

That night I could not fall asleep for a long time. My apologies to the world honored shade and the intimate conversations with my better self lasted and lasted. But then I suddenly thought of those rare 12 spoken words and passed to the land of dreams.

It is clear that Ganz was enchanted by the entire experience, and this is the earliest reference for Ganz's interaction with a national figure in America. He had become a citizen during the Coolidge administration, and this document almost certainly dates from after his visit to play at The White House on January 17, 1929, for Coolidge's last state dinner. At this event, he played a nocturne, two waltzes, and a scherzo of Chopin and ended with the Liszt *Polonaise in E major*.[23]

Naturalization

In 1944, Ganz wrote the following document about his naturalization in 1925. It is equally, and arguably unnecessarily, effusive. Like his article, 'No War Propaganda – And a Great Conductor' (see below), he made his patriotic sentiments and loyalties unequivocally clear. In both instances, he revisits a past event as an immigrant to explain what it meant to him and why it remained significant.

This text may have served as a public talk or possibly as part of his unfinished autobiography. As is typical of Ganz's unpublished papers and talks, there is a sharpened tone at times and, in this instance, as someone who had seen war close at hand, a strong sense of the rights of the individual. In this case, he portrays himself as a proud American but also a man with a strong independent Swiss identity and a sense of personal integrity. This document is multi-layered, beginning with the statement that the 'freedom of Switzerland is over 560 years old' and had been hard won despite its small military forces, thus observing the power of the smaller nation over the larger one and the longer respective history of Switzerland.

The timing of Ganz's naturalization is especially interesting. The very public Muck scandal concerning the National Anthem had resulted in Muck's internment in 1918. At that point, the process for an alien, such as Ganz, requesting citizenship required the initial filing of a declaration of intention to seek citizenship. The applicant could then petition the court in the following two to seven years. If the Muck scandal had alerted Ganz to the fragility of the citizenship process and also the perception of foreign-born musicians, then it is highly likely that he sought to acquire citizenship at the earliest possible opportunity which this alignment of dates suggests. Bearing this in mind, it is unsurprising that members of the St. Louis Symphony Orchestra's board accompanied him to the citizenship ceremony. He demonstrated his fealty to his adopted homeland on a personal as well as a professional level. But despite this, there is nonetheless a pervading tone of making decisions 'on my terms' that is persistent in the document, suggesting that despite the politically charged climate, he nonetheless wanted to assert the independence he was familiar with as a Swiss citizen. The naturalization was all the more public because it aligned with the St. Louis contract signing.

The reference to 'an enthusiastic American' who remarks that if one were not to be American he would happily be Swiss may well be a fictional anecdote. If not, then Ganz's penchant for detail would have provided a name, perhaps age, and greater context. The statement is after all clearly complimentary. Ganz, though, shifts the focus by not describing Switzerland as 'beloved' himself but rather in the words of an American, and this only contributes to the relative opaqueness of the statement. He speaks highly of his homeland but in the safe voice of an(other) American. Overall, he stresses a binary situation of the small but honorable homeland versus the expansiveness of the States while countering many typical misunderstandings. The most critical of these is the reference that a Swiss citizen cannot relinquish citizenship without appealing to the Swiss parliament. This may seem a triviality but whether to request or 'require' the relinquishing of foreign citizenship is a critical distinction between the United States and other countries. The same applies to the home country as some nations do not allow their citizens to obtain a second passport. As such, Ganz points out that he is not relinquishing his home citizenship – and the tone infers that he has no intention of doing so in any event – but rather acquiring a second citizenship that is allied to his thoughts and a 'matter of the heart rather than of the head'. It is fair to suggest that he was not blind to the professional benefits of remaining in the States, hence the presence of the orchestra's administration.

The last paragraph is the most visceral, especially in comparison to the overarching measure and tenor of Ganz's writings. It is also in marked contrast to his writing of The White House visit roughly twenty years earlier. Far from being deferential and overawed by which entrance he would enter at The White House, he instead comments that he is now happy because of his freedom to criticize the government. One might have expected Ganz to comment that he was pleased to be able to vote or perhaps jokingly, pleased to be able to vote, having paid taxes for so long, but instead he stresses his desire, or at least his ability, to criticize the government. Given the devastation of World War I, the need to hold political leaders to account may have been foremost in his mind given his earlier references to Swiss independence.

The customary euphoria following the ceremony and the presence of a photographer 'seeking a picture' of the new American citizen who conducts the city's orchestra would have been professionally astute for Ganz to participate in. As he wrote, he was 'not in the mood' for a photo and there is no reason to believe this wasn't a sincere sentiment, even though there is no commentary on why that would have been the case, such as a delay in the day's proceedings. Given his statement that 'gossip-hungry interviewers insisted upon some highfalutin patriotic statement' and 'threatened' when one wasn't provided, it may have been that personally, the ceremony was not exactly what he thought it would be. The use of the word 'threatened' is a specific example of Ganz carefully choosing his words as he clarifies his own position but also alerts the reader or listener to the feelings he experienced. For Ganz, to pledge allegiance to a country that was not the one of his birth less than ten years after a war that had a pronounced impact on his home country cannot have been easy. It is conceivable that what began as a decision based on professional and financial security was ultimately tougher to digest, especially when an overt show of patriotism in a public forum was expected. This view is reinforced in a story of a student who was nervous about what to play for Ganz when he first encountered him for a lesson in the United States. His reply? 'Play your National Anthem!'[24] and thus show your true (rather than adopted) identity. With regard to the comment that no picture should be taken because it could not be taken of his heart, a reader can infer numerous possible reasons although the comparatively sanguine nature of the document in contrast to The White House visit suggests that Ganz was either still emotionally torn or indeed felt 'threatened'. That he still relayed the story in this fashion in 1944, further reinforces that he feared what the outcome of a second world war would provoke for immigrants in America. There had already been one Red Scare, and he was frequently misidentified. As such, Ganz established his American identity for professional and personal reasons of necessity, and meanwhile, he maintained his Swiss independence in his 'heart'. The tone has a double veil of patriotism.

Naturalization [1944]

Rudolph Ganz

> An enthusiastic American who spent all his summer in his "beloved" Switzerland, as he called it, one day said to his Swiss friend, "If I were not an American, I surely would want to be a Swiss." Whereupon the other answered him, "Same here. If I weren't a Swiss, I certainly would want to be a Swiss." To pass from Swiss to American citizenship is a painless operation. A matter of the heart rather than of the head and of general habits. The freedom of Switzerland is over 560 years old. Many bloody wars were fought between the heavily armed Aggressor Nations surrounding the little mountain republic and its only lightly armed, untrained but brave defenders. He who is willing to die for the preservation of his home and his way of living, will always win out in the end. Swiss history proves it. And the mighty neighbours know it.
>
> Upon signing my record three-year contract as conductor of The St. Louis Symphony Orchestra I decided to become an American Citizen on official paper. I felt that I had been one for many, many years as far as my

spirit[ual?] life activities and look [views] into the future were concerned. I am not a friend of the flag-waving except in the presence of the Enemy or his equal, the two-faced acquaintance. Two of my very good friends of The St. Louis Symphony Board accompanied me to The Federal Court. I had to account for my whereabouts and doings in the war-months in 1914. Our family had been summering that year in Clareus on beautiful Lake Geneva. August first is the most important Swiss National Holiday. It is their "Fourth of July." But it also was the day of the annual artist gathering at the home of Paderewski in Morges.

Then, suddenly, the church bells ringing, alarm, drummers and town criers rushing thru the streets of the little town ...WAR ...WAR! The first World war was on its way. Swiss mobilization was on immediately. No Swiss could leave his home!

I was too young to be scrapped and too old to be in the regular Army. My first and last Army service had been in 1897. That short training period to which every young able-bodied Swiss has to submit has been a blessed guide during my entire life, because it taught me the meaning of discipline, of brotherhood, of camaraderie, of tolerance and understanding of the "lesser" type. Let us hope and pray that our America will institute some universal military training when World-War II comes to its victorious end.

[Following the naturalization ceremony]

... I happily shook hands with my newly acquired compatriots of the St. Louis Symphony Board. When I reached the Lobby I was face to face with a row of newspaper reporters and a cameraman.

They heard an official say to me: 'please sign here, and here, and here... and now read what Uncle Sam has to say to all Swiss citizens after they have received their Naturalization papers'. This special document is a curious one. A Swiss cannot lose his citizenship unless they appear before The National Parliament and ask for its revocation. Uncle Sam insists upon honoring this unusual situation but requests that their new American citizen refuse to pay military taxes in the land of his birth. And how easy it was to make such a promise.

I refused to be photographed since the man could not take a picture of my heart. The gossip-hungry interviewers insisted upon some highfalutin patriotic statement from this most recent North American. I was not in the mood. They threatened despite my assurances that I had been a good American in spirit ever since I reached these shores. Finally I gave in and satisfied their curiosity. "I am happy to be an American Citizen because now I can criticize The Government," I said. Were they satisfied?!?[25]

RG 4/3 1944

Ganz had become a citizen in 1925, and the development of his career in the United States was steadily paced while his popularity continued to increase, not least with fellow musicians. When he resigned from his post with the

St. Louis Orchestra in 1927, forty-two musicians of the orchestra signed a letter that expressed the depth of feeling engendered by his tenure. In September of the same year, he moved to New York City and also performed with the New York Philharmonic. In 1928, he moved permanently to Chicago.

The letter sent to him from the orchestra shows the lengths to which Ganz went to collaborate with numerous professional organizations, not least those devoted to education. It is striking that the Young People's Concerts are mentioned as a key point of his success in the city, as this work was to be a developing theme of his long career. His programs with the orchestra had built a national reputation, and the *Musical Courier* noted that 'what Ganz has been doing to build up interest in music in St. Louis is not a matter of question but of history'.[26] The *St. Louis Post Dispatch* went still further, commenting that 'there have been minutes that took us into the fourth dimension – minutes of serene and pensive beauty – poignant minutes – iridescent minutes – minutes of tumultuous despair'.[27] Ganz had always placed – and increasingly focused attention on – the younger generation to move the profession and the cultural life of cities forward. Children are of course remarkably open to new ideas and do not embody the prejudices that so often impede adults. Although managerial difficulties and Ganz's perception of a lack of business acumen on the part of the orchestra's executive body influenced his decision to leave, the press – though supportive of Ganz – portrayed the realities of working in a city where programming had traditionally been conservative. Ganz had the strong support of both musicians and critics. In the *Christian Science Monitor*, it was noted that:

> Mr. Ganz has impressed upon the orchestra a very high type of musical culture. He has lifted it out of a certain naïve provincialism and given it a sound cosmopolitanism. The conservative element in St. Louis, of which there is something of a preponderance, has steadily fought this very desirable expansion.[28]

Pierre Key's writing in an editorial for *Musical Digest* had a still more acuminate edge to it:

> … St. Louis displayed a horizon of thought and action which at times became dwarfed almost to invisibility…Perhaps one day St. Louisans will appreciate more clearly what Rudolph Ganz did for their city.[29]

The letter from the orchestra enumerates the qualities that enabled Ganz's tenure to remain cherished among the city's professional musicians, with particular reference to his promotion of American musicians and his collaboration with prominent American institutions. This approach to the profession and his life in America is noteworthy because he could easily have programmed easy-listening classics for the orchestra but instead sought to expand the repertoire, educate children and thus gain the support of their parents, and advance the work of American musicians, including contemporary composers.

Letter to Ganz from Musicians of the St. Louis Symphony Orchestra [extract]
March 16, 1927

> You have certainly encouraged American composers considerably by giving them opportunities of hearing their own works. Likewise, American and particularly local soloists have been greatly encouraged by you. In fact, your generous spirit of co-operation with such organizations as Washington University, St. Louis University, the Musicians Guild, Piano Teachers' Educational Association, Community Music School's Foundation, Mu Phi Epsilon Sorority, and others and above all your great success with the young peoples' concerts has endeared you beyond words, to your many loyal supporters.

Music and Patriotism

As noted above, throughout Ganz's life in America, there were uncomfortable moments when he was identified as German rather than Swiss. Even though his speaking accent was gentle, and his command of English was exceptional and possessed a strong command of nuance and humor, this was a point he was especially sensitive to. In 1927, two years after Ganz became a US citizen, the Swiss American Historical Society was founded in Chicago. The initiators of the SAHS, Ernest A. Kübler, Bruno Bachmann, and August Rüedy, were among those who 'were annoyed and concerned' ... 'by the fact that every outstanding person of Swiss origin was claimed by some other nation'.[30] The group's goal was scholarly, although no academicians were initially among them. The members published a book in 1932 titled Prominent Americans of Swiss Origin. It featured seventy-one personalities grouped into eleven categories: Pioneers, Theologians, Soldiers, Statesmen, Physicians and Surgeons, Industrialists, Merchants, Bankers; Scientists, Journalists, and Engineers.[31] There appeared to be very little interest in the larger humanities and no mention of musicians at all. Moreover, there was no mention of the society in Ganz's papers, which fortifies the argument that he really did see himself as a new man in America and was keen to leave some aspect of his European past behind him. The following article by Ganz demonstrates the very careful path he took between the professional and the public persona. He did not give way to professional criticism or gossip easily in his writings, but his sensitivity to the issue of his relationship with the conductor Karl Muck is one that clearly rankled him, so much so that he should not simply mention it in passing within the context of another writing or talk but instead devote an entire article written more than twenty years later to circumstances surrounding an event that upset him. The title – presumably by Ganz and not the publication's editor – demonstrates this very succinctly.

First, given the writer and the publication, the statement that war and music do not comingle and, second, that he is about to discuss a revered figure is intriguing. The article is very out of character for Ganz's public persona and utterly unapologetic while also being multi-layered. Throughout the text, Ganz speaks glowingly of Muck's musical abilities, a point that Ganz's and Muck's professional colleagues attest to. However, the narrative is interlaced with private information as the 'American Ganz' speaks of the Old World of Europe and provides insider anecdotes. The consequence of this is the portrayal of a colossal fall from grace by Muck in Ganz's eyes, but by speaking of Muck's musical abilities he also establishes why he was in contact with him at all at an earlier time. Whereas Ganz had made a pilgrimage to hear Muck conduct in Boston, he could not let go of seeing Muck wearing the cuff buttons with the Kaiser's 'W' emblazoned on them or his criticism of Debussy. Ironically, it is Ganz who takes issue with the gossipy nature of Muck's 'news' of the German forces' discovery of information about Belgian-British treaties when in fact the tone of Ganz could equally be described as manipulative.

The influence of Muck in Boston musical life is clearly seen by Ganz to be a privilege that Muck should have been grateful for. That a US major should directly request the release of Muck from his military obligations in order to fulfill his commitments in Boston may seem extraordinary, although clearly it was a successful request. Ganz rightly notes that Muck did conduct the American National Anthem without issue many times.

It is interesting to observe that when Ganz describes his mounting fury at Muck's gossiping, he uses the description 'timpani and gran casa joined in the crescendo,' which, coincidentally, is one of his many complaints about poor arrangements of the anthem, as will be discussed later. The final sentences are especially damning coming from the generally diplomatic and avuncular Ganz. He suggests that Muck got entirely what he deserved – 'too many Germans' in the internment camp – and – artfully placed to end on the higher note of art – that Debussy lives on. The double blow seals the critique while also positioning Ganz as someone who is not only removed from the situation as a Swiss, and now also an American citizen, but as a man of higher morals and ethics, as the praise in the conclusion of the letter from the St. Louis musicians (above) alludes to.

The Muck scandal that resulted in his internment in 1918 was well known by the time of Ganz's article and has been studied at length in the writings of Melissa D. Burrage, E. Douglas Bomberger, Edmund A. Bowles, Irving Lowens, and Matthew Mugmon.[32] However, Ganz stays clear of the developments, misunderstanding, and hysteria surrounding the Muck scandal and instead dwells on personal anecdotes. He portrays Muck as a significant musical force that he made a 'pilgrimage' to hear conduct in Boston and who he happily worked with. But he selectively relays the details of Muck's career in this article. This is important to note because this was a published document by a musician and administrator (Ganz) who was a highly respected figure at this stage of his career. His summary of the incident aligns with a comment of

Boston's mayor in 1917, James Michael, who stated that 'Dr. Muck and his patron, Major Higginson, have sacrificed their artistic spirits to public sentiment'.[33] With this article, Ganz made a point to do the very opposite. Moreover, he discussed historic wrongdoing within the timeframe of World War I in a document published during World War II.

Ganz does not mention that Muck had offered to step down as director of the Boston Symphony Orchestra at the beginning of the war because, though Swiss, he had largely worked in Germany. Further, Ganz asserts that, with the cuff buttons emblazoned with the Kaiser's 'W', Muck can only be considered a 'loyal German'. He also attacks Muck for being an unprofessional gossip.

Most critically, and here the past comes to the contemporary and connects the larger narrative of Ganz and the National Anthem, he attacks Muck on the grounds on which he can most uncontestably assert his own voice – musical matters. He takes issue with the fact that the version Muck conducted of the National Anthem was by Victor Herbert, with its 'academic German counterpoint' as *The New York Times* had commented.[34] Herbert was born on Guernsey (although his mother told him he was born in Dublin) and had studied in Stuttgart. After moving to New York City in 1886, he was employed by Walter Damrosch at the Metropolitan Opera and was active in the German musical community of the city. However, the issues of 'German' counterpoint were to become a constant source of commentary for Ganz and would ultimately be directed at Damrosch's own version.

No War Propaganda – And a Great Conductor Rudolph Ganz

Musical Facts, July–August, 1940[35]

> *Editor's Note: In the May issue of MUSICAL FACTS, there appeared an article by Herbert F. Peyser titled "War Propaganda—and a Great Conductor", which was a note on the various events which led to the internment in 1917 of Karl Muck, Conductor of the Boston Symphony Orchestra. The article was timely and most appropriate in these days of war-hysteria and uncertainty. Since MUSICAL FACTS opened this subject, it would not be well to close it without presenting the highly illuminating facts which Dr. Ganz has contributed. Here is a valuable addendum to the Muck legend, even though it may tarnish the halo of martyrdom which time and an apologetic America have placed above Muck's head.*
>
> In 1917 I did something of which I am not ashamed despite the fact that some people may think I should be. Before 1917 I considered Karl Muck one of the great conductors of our generation, and today, in 1940, I still feel the same way about him who passed away a short time ago. My admiration for the musician Muck never suffered; despite the unpleasant and entirely unnecessary event which was forced upon me by the man or, I must say, "German," Muck.

An Immigrant's Perspective – The Role of Public Patriotism

We had known each other in Berlin for many years prior to my final departure from Germany in July 1914. We were often together at parties, and I gladly confess to a weakness of seeking conversation with a highly interesting, somewhat fascinating, older colleague. However, we often clashed on minor matters like cuffbuttons [sic] or Debussy. He admitted that he did not care for the French Master's impressionistic music, but he thought that audiences were entitled to become acquainted with his works. And he gave finely rehearsed, colorful, meticulous performances that spoke volumes for the conductor's artistic integrity. I well remember the evening when I found fault with, or took exception to, his royal cuff buttons consisting of heavily bejeweled "W's" (-Wilhelms-). This, however, only after he had tried to assure me that he was a *landsmann* (a compatriot) of mine.

Now, Karl Muck was born in Darmstadt (Germany). His father is said to have lived in Zug (Switzerland) for many years, and I learned that young Karl went to school there, up to the time when he began his University studies in Germany. There was, therefore, some Swiss atmosphere, perhaps even real Swiss mountain-air, around him in his early days. Years later he opera-conducted at the Municipal Theatre in Zürich. The above-mentioned cufflinks were a gift from the imperial hand after Muck had become chief conductor at the Royal Opera House in Berlin in 1892. This position could not be held by anyone but a German, and a really devoted German at that.

I always enjoyed Dr. Muck's biting repartee and cynical smile; the memory of every professional cooperation with him and the grand Boston Symphony Orchestra as well as our many social [encounters] (except the last one) are very dear to me. I had the privilege of being the soloist in Chicago in 1907 or 1908 when the Bostonians filled the Auditorium Theatre on the occasion of their local debut. I appeared often under his inspiring leadership in Boston and other New England cities. I often pilgrimaged to Boston Symphony Hall to hear his concerts.

Returning to the U.S.A. in the last week of September 1914 (after having been mobilized in the Swiss Army for four weeks), I was informed, by friends who were supposed to know, that Major Higginson[36] had written to the Kaiser that, unless he would release Dr. Muck from his military duties as a *landstrum*-soldier (the oldest clan of reserves) doing duty somewhere near the Festspielhaus in Bayreuth and let him return to Boston to conduct the Symphony seasons, he would dissolve the organization for which he had been the grand and generous sponsor. Dr. Muck arrived in Boston. I daresay that it must have been rather hard for him to face the already pronounced pro-ally temperature of the good old Bostonians. I left New York hurriedly to be present at the opening of the Boston season. I was among those who were asked please to rise at his entrance and stand until the entire audience had done likewise. And we did make an effort to give the icy and pale looking delegate of the Kaiser as warm a welcome as it was possible when all concerned felt that things were just not right.

The concert came off beautifully. The [Liszt] *Mephisto Waltz* was never more diabolical and made an appropriate exit for the unhappy conductor. With my old friend and colleague Stasny, I reached the Green Room where I was an unwilling witness to a lot of meaningless handshaking and many a mysterious mumbled word between members of the board and the director. While accepting the tepid compliments from the visitors, Muck whispered to me: 'Ganz, stay, I have important news for you!' I wondered.

Stasny and I waited until everyone had left. Then came the information: "My ambassador in Washington, Graf Bernsdorf, writes me today that the German troops in Belgium have found all the papers pertaining to the secret treaties between England and Belgium, etc…". And he frolicked over the "exciting" bit of news. The complete neutrality of my facial expression seemed to upset him. He suddenly swerved in front of me and, with a, should I say, rather unfriendly look, threw the following sentence at ne: "Aha, you are not interested – I should have known…you are Swiss… THEY do not know where they belong…", "Yes, *I* do know" was my cold and only answer. Timpani and gran casa joined in the crescendo of his verbal attack and the unavoidable climax was reached in a word which could hardly apply to me. I bowed politely, silently, neutrally, and left.

I never saw Dr. Muck again. The sour note preceding my departure from the Green Room was recorded in my ear, however. You do not forget moments like that one.

1917 came. Dr. Muck was asked to conduct the 'Star Spangled Banner' when the orchestra gave a concert in Providence (R.I). He did not refuse, as I learned afterwards. It was Major Higginson himself who prevented the playing of the National Anthem by saying that it did not belong in a Symphony program. (Remember the Toscanini-Mussolini incident at the Scala?) The Carnegie Hall audience in New York let it be known through the local press that they would insist on the playing of the anthem. I sympathized with Muck. No one should have expected a loyal German to conduct what was sacred to the then enemy. But Muck *DID* conduct it with what some New York papers called 'academic German counterpoint'.[37]

Poor Muck! He could have replied – but he did not – that the transcription, 'transfiguration' or better disfiguration of the 'national' bass of the anthem was the well-meant 'scientific' elaboration of one Victor Herbert. At a recent concert in the Young Peoples Series of the New York Philharmonic I had programmed the 'American Fantasy' of Herbert but requested the orchestra to ignore the 'contrapunting' finale above mentioned and to perform the simple, known, and accepted version of the 'Star Spangled Banner' to the enthusiastic singing of the young audience. I may have conservative ideas about National Anthems. I am in favor of the spiritual firing squad for anyone tampering with them melodically, harmonically, or rhythmically.

One day, on my way from New York to Chicago, Judge Mack called to see me from his table in the dining car: "I see by the paper that your countryman Dr. Muck has been arrested". My countryman!! My *Landsmann!* What with the cuffbuttons, [*sic*] 'his' German ambassador getting secret information...At once I wired to the Swiss Minister in Washington protesting against the alleged Swiss citizenship of my former friend and offering evidence to justify my protest. A few days later the representative of the Swiss Government in the U.S.A. let it be known that he was not interested in Dr. Muck's assertion of Swiss citizenship.

In the concentration camp at Fort Oglethorpe Dr. Muck found a temporary home. From there he wrote an illustrated postcard to his old friend, Chadwick, in Boston. Chadwick showed me the card, and did we enjoy the dear good Doctor's delightful information regarding his surroundings. It certainly diluted, if not sweetened, the sour note of days gone by.

The message spoke of 'the nice room, the lovely view from its window, of the beautiful Steinway at his personal disposal, of the unsuccessful attempts of a colleague who wanted to play four hands, of the meals that were good and plenty'...and *now*, listen, dear reader (if you have had patience to stay with me)...what a finale of "the only disagreeable thing about the place – *the presence of too many Germans.*'

***

Debussy lives. The cuffbuttons [*sic*] have gone out of fashion.

Although the anti-German sentiment that was rife during World War I was less pronounced in World War II, critics were also keen to note the benefits to American musicians as Ganz does in the subsequent article, *Music in the threatened areas*. *Newsweek* ran an article in 1939 with the headline 'War expected to make U.S. World's Music Center' and the following text:

Today, with Europe's musicians reaching for guns instead of violins and trumpets, with opera houses and concert halls dark in many foreign cities, the United States is expected to experience an even bigger music boom. Professional and trade leaders predict that the war may make America the world's music leader.[38]

Olin Downes wrote that it was a 'blessing' that for the 1942–1943 season the Metropolitan Opera had only engaged American singers, whereas they had previously engaged singers from abroad for principal roles.'[39]

Ganz's text, *Music in the threatened areas*, is a typed document within his papers that at first appears to be a speech. He initially acknowledges that he is not present to give the talk, and so as this relates specifically to Chicago, it is quite possible that it was either delivered by someone on his behalf or recorded as a radio statement. There is a very subtle and indeed savvy manipulation of the evidence he presents to further his arguments. To begin, he sets out his own position and professional standing, noting his affiliations with the leading orchestras of New York City and San Francisco. He then states that music in nearly all genres – he does not mention opera, which for Ganz is a consistent omission and perhaps because of the international nature of many casts – had continued to be performed despite the war effort. Further, concert attendance had been very high, and both professional organizations (such as the orchestras) and the amateur choral societies had all 'fared equally well'. He then clarifies that this is in part because of the resilience of the public, who, even though they are aware that a performance might be disrupted by an emergency situation, decide to carry on with their business, nonetheless.

The statement of 'unity through music' was adopted at the Board of Directors' meeting of the Music Educators National Conference (MENC) in October 1940. In 1941, a committee on 'American Unity Through Music' was formed with personnel from MENC, the Music Teachers National Association, and the National Association of Schools of Music.[40] The committee produced a report that was published in the March/April edition of the *Music Educators Journal* that included the following statement:

> Music is a vital factor in building a state of mind and heart which is essential to American spirit and morale, to worthy pride in things which are American, and to the confidence and assurance necessary to full appreciation, protection and maintenance of the American Way of Life. To this end, upwards of 45,000 school and college music leaders are intensifying their organized programs of music activities, not only in the schools and colleges, but in every sphere of our social structure.[41]

The committee stressed the importance of singing patriotic songs, including the National Anthem, 'fervently' in the classroom, at assemblies and public performances, and further encouraged the use of folk and pioneer songs which were to be distributed via the committee with the assistance of the chief of the music division of the Library of Congress. Flag raising and lowering ceremonies were increasingly accompanied by music in many schools, and community parades 'often include bands playing rousing patriotic songs and marches'.[42] Publishers across the country were also engaged in providing anthologies of patriotic songs both of the United States and 'Our Allies,' although, as Amy Beegle notes, these sometimes included songs that did not originate in the countries they were categorized under.[43] Music educators who attended the National Institute on Music Education in Wartime, held in Chicago in November 1942, heard commentaries from John W. Beattie, dean of the School of Music at Northwestern University, and Roy D. Welch, chairman of the Music Department at Princeton University, as well as representatives of government departments and key figures from the world of radio broadcasting, music instruction, and other state music associations.[44]

In 1943, Charles Seeger published an article titled 'Wartime and Peacetime Programs in Music Education' for the *Music Educators Journal* based on a statement at the 1942 gathering. He suggested that greater attention needed to be paid to collaboration between music educators and composers living in the United States, whether born on US soil or immigrants noting possible collaboration and improvement between the 'so-called prestige fields such as the virtuoso and his circle, fine-art composition and its audience, musicology, [and] general scholarship…'.[45] He further promoted the idea that music was more than just 'good in itself' and rather 'good for something' and that:

> after a century of music as the 'art of peace' and 'universal harmony,' we are pressing it as a weapon in war – and at that not only as a defensive weapon for the home front but as an offensive one in the armed services![46]

In a complementary vein, Ganz was concerned with both portraying his clear identity as an immigrant – a role that Seeger valued – that could respond to the challenges being faced and his public contribution to the larger American war effort. The article captures the important contemporary discussion of morale and music and, most significantly, bolsters Ganz's advancing cause of patriotic music through his work on the National Anthem.

In his text, Ganz underlines the words 'to best serve the men in uniform' …'doing their sacred duty' and portrays the work on the battlefield in noble terms. He offers his skills both as an administrator and as a concert artist in free programs – notably not seeking to profit from the war effort – but then, after previously stressing the importance of promoting music 'from Symphony to Swing,' he dismissively refers to the so-called popular music while noting that everyone has personal tastes. His final sentences once again refer to the importance of Morale (Ganz's uppercase usage) for those who are soon to be in battle while thinking with 'pride' of those that are already on the battlefield. As such, the larger musical argument is veiled in a patriotism that extends beyond musical matters as Ganz shows himself to be more than just a musician, but also a citizen who understands the consequences of war. The earlier perception of Karl Muck as undeserving is contrasted here with a view that not only shows loyalty to the country but also shows admiration for service. As the military will fight in the theatre of war, so too Ganz will offer his artistic contribution which, as Seeger noted, was critical to the larger effort.

This clear expression of American patriotism at a critical moment in history might have seemed essential and even personally and professionally beneficial to Ganz. I have noted above how Ganz felt 'threatened' (*Naturalization*) by the aspects of not adhering to expected public patriotism in St. Louis and the title of this article uses the same language. It would certainly have been welcomed in the higher social circles that he frequented in order to attract support for his endeavors as well as the institutional centers that are critical to the workings of the profession at large. As discussed earlier, Bomberger's[47] research on the xenophobic approach of *The Chronicle* and its reach into society circles cannot be underestimated given the success of their anti-German agenda. Equally, Ganz may have felt that this was an opportunity to reinforce the importance of Chicago's place in the national landscape and, in no small measure, his own place in the musical pantheon and national discourse. But as an immigrant, he also places himself squarely in a sphere of positive influence during a time of war. Critically, he writes this only months after the attack on Pearl Harbor. As Annegret Fauser has noted, this moment in history had a profound impact on the growth of patriotic concerns. Eleanor Roosevelt's letter, published in *Musical America* in 1942 (Figure 1.1), urged Americans to make music because it was 'one of the finest flowerings of that free civilization which has come down to us from our liberty loving forefathers'.[48]

Further, the presentation of music on United Service Organizations (USO) tours 'became a badge of honor for musicians engaged in the more official duty of war entertainment'.[49] However, the spirit of advancement within the profession often led to competitive turf wars. Meetings at the house of Walter Damrosch, in January 1941 (a month after the Pearl Harbor attack):

> pitted the meeting's organizer, the composer Samuel Barlow (head of the Independent Citizens Committee for the Arts, Sciences, and Professions in New York and a regular contributor to Modern Music), against several other representatives of musical organizations, including Aaron Copland (for the American Composers Alliance), Edwin Hughes (President of the National Music Council), Horace Johnson (New York [Works Progress Administration]), Jacob Rosenberg (Local 802 of the American Federation of Musicians [AFM]), and Blanche Witherspoon (for USO camp shows)[50]

as different agendas and personalities maneuvered for their own positions and interests. When Ganz refers to the 'morale of the people', he is referring to the musical 'force for morale' that Eleanor Roosevelt had written about. Once again, he carefully aligns himself on the safest side of political debate.

Figure 1.1 Eleanor Roosevelt, 'Music Should Go On! A Message from the First Lady' (1950).

Music in the Threatened Areas [1942]
Rudolph Ganz

Ladies and Gentlemen:

I deeply regret my inability to be present at tonight's meeting, but I want to assure you that I am with you in spirit though I am some 2300 miles away from Chicago as to distance. Having been active in concert work during the last four months on both the Atlantic and Pacific Coast, I feel that I can speak of "Music in the Threatened Areas" with the authority that comes from one's own experience.

All the regular concerts of the New York Philharmonic Society and the San Francisco Symphony Orchestra as well as the Series of Young People's and Children's Concerts offered by these two organizations (and which I have the honor and pleasure of serving as permanent conductor) are given in large halls and were either sold out or had nearly capacity audiences. Attendance at recitals of well-known singers and instrumentalists has been splendid, and other musical events presented by other organizations, chamber music groups, choral societies, etc., have fared equally well.

These facts speak highly of the evident confidence the people of these two cities have in the preparedness of their civilian defense because an air-raid alarm followed by a complete black-out might occur at any moment. Nowhere have I found any nervousness among the people and yet I have met many from all walks of life, men and women, civilians and soldiers. Most of them realize the seriousness of the situation, the changes brought about by the emergency, the uncertainty of the immediate future. But they all believe in the final victory of our case which is: Right before Might.

I therefore dare say that the Morale of the people in the threatened areas, as I have seen it, is excellent and might easily serve as an example for us here in Chicago where there is still so much evidence of isolating and isolated sentiment. Let us organize with force and discipline and create unity in cooperation so as to be absolutely sure of constructive results. Danger to our city may be far off, but it is not out of the realm of possibility or probability that we Chicagoans will have to share in the experiences of war as other localities no doubt will.

We must keep music in the foreground of all entertainments, for both civilians and soldiers. Music is the universal language that both old and young, man and woman can understand. By that I mean: music from <u>Symphony to Swing</u>. Music can serve all grades of understanding, all tastes, all likes. First of all: There should be full houses for our wonderful Chicago Symphony Orchestra, our successfully re-animated Chicago Civic Opera, and also for the important and attractive series of concerts offered by different organizations. Music alone can provide that unfailing spiritual life which we need in the present emergency. Music can best fill some of the empty hours of leisure and relaxation.

In addition, let us organize and map out plans how <u>to best serve the men in uniform</u> who are doing their sacred duty by their country and <u>our</u> country, and by their people, our people of the U.S.A. I am anxious to serve on the Committee of Planning, and I am willing to offer my services as a concert artist on programs given free to men in the Army and Navy. There are thousands who will come and hear so-called serious music. Hundreds of thousands will flock to entertainments of so-called popular music. There is a tune for every human being. Once this committee of planning has been formed, musically inclined liaison-officers from every camp should be contacted for immediate organization.

We can think with pride of those who are far away from us, fighting our battles. That's all we can do. So let us be friendly to those who are getting ready to join their brothers-in-arms and entertain them as best we can in their free moments. This is our modest share in building up <u>their</u> Morale as well as ours.

Rudolph Ganz
President of Chicago Musical College

En route
April 6, 1942

In the same year as *Music in the Threatened Areas*, the composer William Grant Still (who corresponded with Ganz about his own compositions), wrote the following text:

> We, as Americans, need to become proud of our own achievements in this field and learn more about them. We should adopt our own culture in preference to the culture of any other nation or nations on earth. Now is the time to make a complete swing in that direction. Since it is patriotic to be American, we should let our Americanism extend to every field of endeavor. ... It is worth just as much to our future as carrying a gun against the enemy.
> Music for morale? Certainly. But let it be AMERICAN music![51]

Throughout Ganz's writings and talks, there is a consistent empowerment of American musicians and composers, although his sentiments do not extend to the exclusivity suggested by Still. His only frustrations appear to stem from a lack of advancement in relation to the profession and society as a whole. These views were also shared with his students. Aside from a genuine interest in his adopted country and a certain progressivism in his views on repertoire – which was certainly more developed than many other performing musicians – there was nonetheless a deliberate interest, if not also a possible professional investment, in the promotion of American composers. Ganz spoke of himself as either an American citizen or a citizen of the world and felt that the promotion of music of contemporary composers was essential to the continuance of the profession.

With a life experience that extended beyond North America and with contacts throughout Europe, not least in connection with his concert tours, his voice as a commentator bore a distinguished resonance, especially when considered in tandem with his work as an administrator. His views, though, largely hinged on an idealism toward America affording audiences new opportunities, and the larger profession a new home, in a postwar culture. Aside from his own departure from Europe, he was convinced that after two world wars, the recovery of art in Europe would be slow. But his correspondence across several years also shows a noticeable absence of discussion about repertoire that he did not see as an inheritor of older traditions.

The Second Viennese School, electronic music, aleatoric music, and computer music are all present in the concert programming of others but elicited no commentary in his writings. He frequently mentioned to students that the 'quality' of new works was paramount in their consideration and often passed along scores by American composers to his students, but they were not avant-garde compositions. In every sense, he was furthering the cause of art music in America quite directly by example and by extension of his pedagogical approach. It would be easy to surmise that Ganz was a figure of an older school who simply had no time for new works generally, and yet in his eighties, he was still writing reviews about new piano pieces, providing that he considered them worthy of the historical canon.

Whatever the merits of Ganz's individual decisions may have been, the majority of piano recitals remained very conservative in terms of repertoire, and the presence of even one work by a living composer was rare. Ganz's clear approach to the promotion of tonal repertoire was likely out of fear that more avant-garde works could have alienated the audience from considering new repertoire by other composers. This approach was followed in subsequent decades, and the broadly conservative programming of regional orchestras around the United States in the late twentieth and early twenty-first centuries provides overwhelming evidence of this.

The following article is one of the few texts of Ganz that could have been fully understood by any of his audience constituencies, whether in the form of a public talk, a lecture to musicians, or a radio broadcast. It has a slightly off-the-cuff informality to it and is resonant with strong opinions. The date of the text is unclear, although the opening text gives some indication. Around the end of World War II, Ganz was consistently conducting works of Russian composers, which he refers to in an earlier section of the same document. Ganz suggests that the United States had a very distinctive role to play in the future of Western art music, especially as Europe recovers from the ravages of two world wars. He writes with an argument that many Americans would have found reassuring and promising. Jessica Gienow-Hecht has commented that in the earlier part of the century, Americans had not felt that their cultural achievements matched the successes in other areas of life. The government did not support the arts as European countries did, and a developing antagonism toward German dominance in the field highlighted growing tensions.[52]

Twenty-five years later, there was no longer a fear of German music and musicians in the same way, but the nature of self-doubt and easy criticism along political lines was still present. As nationalistic tendencies had spread in Europe, the question of identity in America was still lingering within the artistic community. Gienow-Hecht notes that there had long been 'an almost religious desire in the quality of a future native school of composition. Indeed, in the imagination of progressive critics, the future American composer gradually assumed messianic dimensions'.[53] Ganz seized on this desire and offered a path forward that was both practical and a demonstration of his own patriotism. The following newspaper review of a concert with the National Symphony Orchestra in 1939 demonstrates Ganz's acute awareness of the role of patriotism only weeks before World War II, whereas the following article, 'Is there an American School of Composers', discusses the unique position he sees for the role of composers in the United States a decade later.

"Rudolph Ganz Cheered Wildly by Watergate Concert Crowd: 6,500 Cheer Ganz at Watergate[.] Conductor Quiets Audience, After 2 Encores, by Playing National Anthem"
The Washington Post [August 14, 1939]

"The Star-Spangled Banner," sung by 6,500 voices and accompanied by the National Symphony Orchestra, was the Watergate audience's farewell last night to Rudolph Ganz after the first open-air concert he has conducted here under fair skies.

When the cheering continued after the second encore, the Swiss-born conductor used a device he had learned in Canada to send the audience home – he asked them to sing the National Anthem. With a shout of approval the crowd rose, all the musicians whose instruments permitted stood, and one man in a canoe stood up and fell out.[54]

Is there an American School of Composers? [late 1940s?]
Rudolph Ganz

As an observer (during practically all of 40 years) of efforts to create "American" music, I can now declare that we have successfully arrived at the end of many kinds of influence that have prevented us from seeing the light of a pure American art expression through music. During the first years after my arrival from Europe I could feel the ebbing of Mendelssohnian and Lisztian influences upon American writers. As early as May, 1901, I had programmed piano pieces by MacDowell, William Mason and William Sherwood. My share in bringing the native composer to the attention of the musical world is a modest one, I know, although, during my St. Louis conductorship of six years, I performed symphonic works of over 60 different American writers. This interest in the native art represents a natural and honest expression of gratitude on my part for the splendid opportunities offered me in the pursuit and evolution of my personal artistic ambitions and endeavors. The Mendelssohnian influence, that is, the sentimental, sweet, homophonic side of it, still vegetates[?][55] in the cheap, amateurish, sexless, watery ballads inspired by commercially profitable ideas and harmonized by unskilled arrangers.

However, when toastmastering [sic] for the Victor Talking Machine Company at a memorable banquet in New York in 1928, I proclaimed as an introductory remark before presenting John Philip Sousa that American music had gone around the world in the form of the famous Lieutenant's stirring marches, that it was again circling the globe with the lively output of Tin Pan Alley, and, finally, that I knew it would, in the not too distant future, go on its third and most important around-the-earth cruise as a purely absolute, independent, powerful symphonic expression. That this moment is near, that it is in sight, is my humble prediction.

What will he say of the present generation of American composers? Deems Taylor, some year ago, suggested in an essay that the American Beethoven may have been born at that moment in Hoboken, New Jersey. An American master born in that suburb of Europe? No! I counter intimated that a small farm ten miles south of Sleepy Eye, Minnesota, might be a better birthplace for that first great American symphonist. Why not? Think of Haydn! Think of all the humble homes of the great masters!

There has come into the present American expression through music a straight-forward simplicity, a natural ruggedness, a desire for brevity, an avoidance of unnecessary complicatedness, a sympathetic search for a new brief, an attitude of courage, integrity and confidence which we may consider a safe guarantee for ultimate success. Echoes of native melodies and dance music as well as of jazz rhythms will always be welcome when artistically presented. After all, they are in the blood of the average American. Our composers of today are writing in the most difficult forms: chamber music, the symphony, the opera. In doing so they challenge the past in a general way and the present (as represented by Europe or by Europeans in the U.S.) in particular.

The evolution of music in our country is being quickened by the influx of refugee-composers from the Old World. What with the creative masters like Schoenberg, Hindemith, Krenek, Toch, Hijman, Korngold, Britten, Boulanger, Castelnuovo-Tedesco, Weinberger and many others installed in American institutions of learning where their genius, talent, professional and other cultural experience[s] and background are bound to bear fruit! What with their new enthusiasm born out of the realization of the opportunities offered them by the land of their adoption! American youth will profit by their counsel and derive inspiration from their [?] activities and the new works conceived on the soil of their new home. And they in turn, these experienced masters, will work with added impetus in their new

An Immigrant's Perspective – The Role of Public Patriotism

surroundings and create values unhampered by political trends, free from dictated coercion and regimentation.

During the past few thousand years the music-center of the world has shifted from Egypt to Greece, from well-known Italian cities to Paris, Vienna, Berlin, London until it finally settled in New York after the First World War. No one can deny the supremacy of the musical life of the great American metropolis. However, other American cities have risen as important musical centers, and the country-at-large has become a musical beehive. The symphony orchestra, the music schools, the choral and chamber music organizations, the radio, the phonograph, the public school music system, all have contributed to the establishment of standards of execution as well as of instruction which point to a future music life in the United States not equaled by any other country in the past.

The chaos in Europe and its repercussion[s] in other parts of the world will delay the art life in all countries affected by the upheaval. However, the arts do not die. So long as there is one human being living endowed with imagination and filled with the desire for self-expression, art will go on!

It is not so long ago that the serious American composer was defined as an individual whose works were seldom, if ever, performed and who therefore could claim income and royalties leading to death and hunger. How this has changed! Today everybody seems to be interested in him. Staunch champions of his worthy cause have come to the fore. Festivals of American music are taking place in all parts of the land. There is hardly a program to be found without the name of a native or naturalized American composer. No greater promise for the immediate future seems possible. Young America is on the way to an absorbingly powerful music life. It seems to harbor the will to lasting leadership. An irresistible desire to express themselves has taken hold of some of our living young masters of music, and they are in my opinion the forerunners, the pioneers, of a coming national American school of composers that is now in the making.

It was at a luncheon offered to Arnold Schoenberg by some Chicago musicians several years ago that I had the privilege of translating for the guests the short speech made by the Austrian Master of 12-tone Independence. He had said that while still in Vienna he had realized what fine orchestras the United States must have, to judge from the excellency of the phonograph records which he had heard; in every phase of the profession; how he had noticed with great joy the spirit of aggressive progress and daring exploration among some of the young native composers; and how he felt that his coming to America was somewhat superfluous![56] This from the most radical writer of music in our time![57]

In this document, Ganz strongly supports the role of the immigrant composer as an essential part of the equation of progress. By doing so, he adopts a diplomatic approach that promotes the value, rather than the earlier fear, of the role of the immigrant. As noted above, the composers he mentions would not, even by contemporary standards, be considered as avant-garde, and some (Britten and Boulanger) did not spend long in the United States, unlike others (Hindemith and Schoenberg) who actually relocated. The writing of this document in the war years is important to consider because Ganz draws a line between the historic legacy of music in America and how the country can serve as a beacon in the future with 'refugee-composers from the Old World' as a constituent part of the musical community. Interestingly, he does not promote his own music, which was less progressive in style than the music of the composers he refers to. But Ganz, a master of subtlety in language, also speaks to the importance of the new environment that immigrant composers will experience in America, 'free from dictated coercion and regimentation'. This is a liberty in his description because the composers he refers to emigrated (or temporarily moved) to America for different reasons. As an example, Britten was not experiencing 'coercion' or 'regimentation' in England but moved as a pacifist. Similarly, when Ganz refers to festivals 'taking place in all parts of the land' and that there is 'hardly a program to be found without the name of a native or naturalized American composer' included, it is a significant exaggeration.

On the contrary, when he comments that 'young America is on the way to an absorbingly powerful music life', the work of his young people's concerts could certainly be seen in this vein. The 'lasting leadership' and the aspect of future progress are of course central to the nature of critical thinking during a war. Ganz draws on this with the added emphasis of an anecdote that Schoenberg felt his place in America was 'superfluous', such was the progressive nature of the musical environment. When Ganz then also adds direct comparison with European musical centers that have a distinct connection for American audiences of Western art music, he draws the reader/listener into an exciting world of future possibilities and the distinct belief that America can forge a path for music 'not equaled by any other country in the past'. Considering these statements in a contemporary context, it is possible to see that when Ganz railed against the Muck scandal and the nature of war propaganda, he was not beyond advancing his own strong patriotic arguments with the sometimes overt promotion of the facts. What Ganz portrays is a halcyon image that, though potentially possible, advances a specific agenda at a time of national anxiety. The statements are not inaccurate, but they are extremely astute politically in the national climate for the furtherance of Ganz's own career and the necessary public identity of Ganz as a loyal immigrant. His greatest sign of loyalty and devotion to his new country was ultimately to be found in his pursuit of a standardized version of the National Anthem.

Ganz's approach to the issues that concerned him is nearly always through a musical lens, and his collected correspondence at the Newberry Library is a testament to a thoughtful musician who genuinely wanted to see society enriched through a love of the musical literature. He did not make negative comments of other performers, and even in the article 'No War Propaganda – And a Great Conductor', he readily points to Karl Muck's musicianship while criticizing his actions, albeit acknowledging the troubling inconsistencies with this public and easily scandalizing narrative. But can Ganz's comments on Muck be seen as anti-German when seen in the context of his other writings or was he simply overtly patriotic in relation to his adopted country?

In reading Ganz's writings, I find no public views that are especially negative even though there are many areas that were of concern to him, as discussed above. He certainly saw the role of the musician as being central to society and his many commentaries in writing and on radio speak to this relationship, especially with regard to new music. The idea of being a 'complete musician' engaged in all aspects of musical life would have been second nature to him from his early years in Europe for pragmatic reasons although less common among his peers in America. But as Europe rebuilt postwar, there is no evidence that Ganz had any strong desire to return to his homeland. His commentaries and determined promotion of American values and music were seemingly as welcomed and acknowledged as they were foreign to a musician who was aware that such sustained displays of public patriotism in his home country would have met with a measure of skepticism and questioning. At times, these commentaries came close to crossing a line of acceptability for his intended audience. His comment on receiving citizenship that he was 'happy to be an American Citizen because now [he could] criticize The Government'[58] and that the 'gossip-hungry interviewers insisted upon some highfalutin patriotic statement' in *Naturalization* demonstrates that acquiring American citizenship was, as it had been for many immigrants, a practical matter for continued residency and not necessarily his first choice; however, he was grateful for the many opportunities that came his way. Ganz had found a path to sustain his musical career, and it clearly involved taking a sustained approach toward public statements of patriotism. In this vein, the criticism of Muck is indeed a criticism of Germany rather than a German musician. It was a commentary for a local audience and bore the tone of berating a colleague who had not followed American expectations. Ganz managed to avoid such censure, and this was in large part by maintaining a balance between respecting the cultural norms of his adopted country, promoting the music of American composers in equal measure to their European counterparts, and staying clear of controversy. This was achieved by being a regular commentator in print, in lectures, and in broadcasts with a message that placed art at the forefront of his interests.

Notes

1. Charles Hopkins, 'Rudolph Ganz,' *Oxford Music Online* (accessed 1 March, 2023).
2. Rudolph Ganz, Letter from Rudolph Ganz to Dr. Howard Hanson. June 15, 1964; Letter from Rudolph Ganz to H. W. Heinsheimer July 26, 1964.
3. Rudolph Ganz, "No War Propaganda – And a Great Conductor," *Musical Facts*, July–August, 1940, 19–21.
4. Jessica C. E. Gienow-Hecht. *Sound Diplomacy: Music and Emotions in Transatlantic Relations, 1850–1920* (Chicago: University of Chicago Press, 2009), 28.
5. Ibid., 112.
6. Ibid., 38.
7. Ibid., 65.
8. Kevin Phillips, *The Cousins' Wars: Religion, Politics, and the Triumph of Anglo-America* (New York: Basic Books, 1999), 564.
9. E. Douglas Bomberger, "Taking the German Muse Out of Music: *The Chronicle* and US Musical Opinion in World War I," *Journal of the Society for American Music*, 14/2 (2020), 141–142.
10. Ibid., 142. See also Edmund Boles, "Karl Muck and His Compatriots: German Conductors in America during World War I (and How They Coped)," *American Music*, 25 (2007), 405–440.
11. Ibid., 141.
12. Ibid., 151.
13. Cleveland Moffett, "There Is Danger in German Music," *The Chronicle 4*, no. 1 (September 1918). Bomberger, "Taking the German Muse out of Music," 152.
14. Mark Clague, *O Say Can You Hear?* (New York: W. W. Norton, 2022), 107.
15. William James Henderson, "Rising Tide of Sentiment against German Music,' *New York Sun*, December 2, 1917. Cited in Bomberger, "Taking the German Muse Out of Music," 154.
16. Clague, *O Say Can You Hear?*, 106. *St. Louis Star*, February 13, 1917, 4. *Sapulpa Herald* (OK), February 22, 1917, 2.
17. "Noted Singers Bring in $45,000 for Old 69th," *The New York Times*, September 23, 1918.
18. Alfred Human, "Ganz Breaks with German Composer," *Musical America*, January 26, 1918 and April 25, 1918. Jeanne Colette Collester, *Rudolph Ganz – A Musical Pioneer* (Metuchen: The Scarecrow Press, 1995), 30.
19. Ibid., 41.
20. The image is not included in this book because the owner of the copyright could not be established and the quality of the image is poor.
21. Annegret Fauser, *Sounds of War: Music in the United States During World War II* (New York: Oxford University Press, 2013), 51.
22. Collester, *Rudolph Ganz*, 86.
23. Robert H. Ferrell, *Grace Coolidge: The People's Lady in Silent Cal's White House* (Lawrence: University Press of Kansas, 2008), 81. https://content.time.com/time/subscriber/article/0,33009,723561,00.html (accessed December 1, 2022).
24. The student wishes to remain anonymous.
25. The first two letters of the final word are unclear.
26. "An Original Idea," *Musical Courier*, May 14, 1925.
27. "Ganz and Young St. Louis," *St. Louis Post Dispatch*, March 16, 1925.
28. "Mr. Ganz Takes Leave of St. Louis Symphony," *The Christian Science Monitor*, March 19, 1927.
29. Pierre Key, *Musical Digest*, March 15, 1972.
30. www.swissamericanhistoricalsociety.org/history/ (accessed March 10, 2022).

31 Ibid.
32 Boles, "Karl Muck and His Compatriots," 405–440; Bomberger, "Taking the German Muse Out of Music," 142; Melissa D. Burrage, *The Karl Muck Scandal: Classical Music and Xenophobia in World War I America* (Rochester, NY: University of Rochester Press, 2019); Irving Lowens, "*L'affaire Muck*: A Study in War Hysteria (1917–1918)," *Musicology*, 1 (1947), 265–274; Matthew Mugmon, "Patriotism, Art, and 'The Star-Spangled Banner' in World War I: A New Look at the Karl Muck Episode," *Journal of Musicological Research*, 33 (2014), 4–26.
33 "Damrosch Too Against Anthem," *New York Evening Sun*, November 1, 1917. Mugmon, "Patriotism, Art, and 'The Star-Spangled Banner' in World War I," 11.
34 "Arrest Karl Muck as an Enemy Alien," *The New York Times*, March 26, 1918, 3.
35 Rudolph Ganz, "Nor War Propaganda," *Musical Facts*, July–August, 1940, 19–21.
36 Henry Lee Higginson was the founder of the orchestra and a major supporter of European music and musicians, which, on occasion, caused him to be criticized for not supporting local musicians.
37 "Arrest Karl Muck as an Enemy Alien," *The New York Times*, March 26, 1918, 3.
38 "War Expected to Make U.S. World's Music Center," *Newsweek*, October 2, 1939. Fauser, *Sounds of War*, 33.
39 Olin Downes, "Opera Opening," *The New York Times*, November 22, 1942. Fauser, *Sounds of War*, 33.
40 Amy Beegle, "American Music Education 1941–1946: Meeting Needs and Making Adjustments during World War II," *Journal of Historical Research in Music Education*, 26/1 (October 2004), 55.
41 "Committee on American Unity Through Music, 'American Unity Through Music,'" *Music Educators Journal*, 27/5 (1941), 10.
42 Beegle, "American Music Education 1941–1946," 56.
43 Ibid., 58.
44 Ibid.
45 Charles Seeger, "Wartime and Peacetime Programs in Music Education," *Music Educators Journal*, 29/3 (1943), 13.
46 Ibid., 12.
47 Bomberger, "Taking the German Muse out of Music," 141–175.
48 Eleanor Roosevelt, "Music Should Go On! A Message from the First Lady," *Musical America*, 62 (February 10, 1942), 3. Fauser, *Sounds of War*, 35.
49 Ibid., 37.
50 Ibid., 65.
51 William Grant Still, "Composer Says 'Lend Lease' in Music Extends to Our Enemies," *Chicago Defender*, October 17, 1942.
52 Gienow-Hecht, *Sound Diplomacy*, 154.
53 Ibid., 162.
54 John Chabot Smith, "Rudolph Ganz Cheered Wildly by Watergate Concert Crowd: 6,500 Cheer Ganz at Watergate Conductor Quiets Audience, After 2 Encores, by Playing National Anthem," *The Washington Post*, August 14, 1939.
55 Begetates (with the 'b' circled by hand).
56 Underlined by hand.
57 Exclamation mark added by hand.
58 The first two letters of the final word are unclear.

2 The National Anthem and the Challenge of Standardization

Ganz was deeply interested in the performance practice of the National Anthem, and it is the most recurring topic in all of his writings. Whether he saw his commitment to seeking a standardized version of the anthem as a specific act of personal patriotism is unknown. However, when considered alongside his writings on America as a beacon for the future of art music in the postwar years, his promotion of American composers, his condemnation of Karl Muck, or his retelling of meeting President Coolidge at The White House, it is highly likely. Many other musical immigrants were very active in the professional musical life of America but did not feel the need to engage in a prolonged discussion with colleagues about a standardized version of the National Anthem. A standardized version would involve an agreed musical text and accompaniment which, to this day, does not exist. As this topic could have potentially been disastrous for Ganz to consider immersing himself in, and he was an astute musician and administrator, I believe he genuinely considered this aspect of his work as either a critical part of his own public patriotism or as the best defense against the criticism that had ruined the careers of many other immigrants, as discussed in Chapter 1.

Central to an understanding of any discussion about versions of the National Anthem is the question of how it is identified as a piece of music. National anthems appear within hymnals that are otherwise filled with standardized musical texts, and the expectation is that they will be performed with the same measure of consistency as the other pieces in the same book. The complicated origins of employing a consistent tune to be used for the 'Star-Spangled Banner' begin with the melody by John Stafford Smith that was written ca. 1773 for the Anacreontic Society in London, first published ca. 1778, and set to the words 'To Anacreon in Heaven'. It later became popular as a banner ballad in America and was used in numerous different texts.

In his research on this tune, Richard Hill questioned whether the words might have been written to a tune that preexisted before its use at meetings of the Anacreontic Society. The triadic nature could have allowed for a performance on a valve trumpet, and therefore, it possibly began life as a military melody.[1] If this were the case, then its eventual use as a national anthem would

DOI: 10.4324/9781003430582-3

be especially intriguing. Sadly, despite Hill's considerable research on this topic, new information came to light shortly after Hill's death with the discovery of a contemporary diary entry by Richard John Samuel Stevens about the Anacreontic Society that he regularly attended. He referred to the Anacreontic Song that Stafford Smith had 'set to music'.[2] However, considering the degree of musical material that was borrowed by composers during this period, does this fully rule out Hill's doubts? Certainly, there is a very strong association with Stafford Smith, but Hill's questioning lay with the absence of a primary source, the assumption of association, the uneven nature of the prosody, and the lack of a later connection to Stafford Smith. Hill did not understand why Stafford Smith would not have acknowledged his authorship of the melody sixty years after composing the tune and twenty-two years after it was associated with the 'Star-Spangled Banner', even though Stafford Smith's glee arrangement (potentially of a work by someone else) had appeared in his *Fifth Book of Canzonets* published in 1799.[3] These sorts of doubts often cause issues with questions of musical authorship, and I believe there remains some truth in Hill's argument that something is either not quite right or that this was an unusual work for Stafford Smith to produce. The lack of ownership that Hill raises is especially significant in this regard.

The song was typically sung at the Society meetings by a professional soloist, with the chorus sung by all present. The piece served as a 'club anthem' that promoted the club's 'dual mission of harmony and fun', and in the context of the meetings, it served as a ritual aspect that moved members from the dining room to a concert space.[4] The tune was used for several sets of words, and as Clague notes, 'when the United States declared war on Britain in June 1812, Anacreontic parodies were deployed to rally the nation [and there were] at least twenty before Key penned his famous one'. When Francis Scott Key picked the same tune for the 'Defence of Fort McHenry', he simply made the obvious choice.[5] Key would likely be very surprised to know that his text had remained popular because banner ballads such as this were used to promote a cause, typically political, and then be replaced with another ballad.

The first sheet music copy of the song, arranged by Thomas Carr of Baltimore, appeared in 1814. Through the many debates that Ganz and others have had concerning how different versions of the tune could be reconciled into one standardized version, this copy has not been a primary source of reference. However, it provides critical answers if an interpretation that is considered 'original' is to be assessed. I shall discuss this later. But here lies the problem. If the nature of the piece was originally dictated by a particular period, should subsequent generations adhere to this or dictate their own performance style or styles? Clague writes that 'the expressive power of Key's song lies in its musical flexibility. To standardize the anthem is to standardize patriotism itself'.[6] However, if an individual interpretation is expected, then the performance is only one of unity by witness rather than by participation. This view can be seen most easily in the difference between a choral piece and a vocal solo. The first is sung by a group, and the latter is sung by one person. The musical interpretation could be significantly different even though the piece is ostensibly the same. But is the individual representing the gathered masses or simply a representative of many individuals? When the piece is sung by a choir, the musical text is effectively determined in advance, and for directors of ensembles, this is presumed. The debate about this contrasting approach between solo and communal singing of the National Anthem continues to this day.

When Henry Higginson, the founder of the Boston Symphony Orchestra, commented in 1917 that the anthem 'had no place in an art concert',[7] he defined the piece as a popular work that was 'fit for concerts of the Boston Pops but not the Boston Symphony Orchestra'.[8] Higginson's view was bolstered by a letter of support from Judge Ebenezer R. Hoar of Concord, Massachusetts, who stated that:

> whatever may be said for the playing of patriotic airs in public gatherings, the Star-Spangled Banner is not well-fitted for a full-string orchestra, good as it is for a military band. The objection to playing it is not in any sense on patriotic grounds, but because of its inappropriateness, and I hope you will not give way.[9]

Clague's view about the 'expressive power' was also noted by William Lichtenwanger when he was asked whether 'America' might be a better alternative as a National Anthem. For him, the power of the 'Star-Spangled Banner' overcame the musical obstacles that had long been the source of complaint. But later in the same article, he also suggested the idea that perhaps the National Anthem could be reserved for special events and 'America' for others:

> ... much as I like that song and would approve of its use on many occasions to avoid overuse of the anthem, there are two overriding reasons why I would deplore "dumping" the SSB in favor of the other. One is that to me the music of THE STAR-SPANGLED BANNER is infinitely more stirring, more plangent than Samuel Ward's nice tune [for America]. It is, in a word not much used these days but surely applicable here, truly grand. It has a proper length, a proper dignity; it has zest and musical pizzazz. The very passage, the high "break" that some people find so intimidating to sing, provides a musical interlude that makes the close all the more thrilling.
>
> Those who call that passage "unsingable" should sing it at the tops of their voices and not worry about the niceties of pitch or vocal quality.[10]

Knowing that the original performances of the tune at meetings of The Anacreontic Society were led by a soloist provides one justification for an individual approach, but the 1814 edition of Thomas Carr, the first known edition to unite the music of 'The Star-Spangled Banner' with the tune, answers many questions if an 'authentic' performance is to be considered (see Figure 2.1).

This version begins with an introduction, which is no longer a common practice, and ends with a brief and distinctive conclusion. There is no descending triad on the first word ('O'), which instead is given a full beat on the same note as the second word ('say'). There are no quick dotted rhythms within beats, whether the pitch is repeated or using a neighboring note. The exception to this can be seen in the concluding accompaniment that does use quick dotted rhythms. When the piece is repeated, the final section is sung as a 'chorus', thus dividing the work between soloist and chorus but expecting the chorus to also sing the higher notes toward the end. The word 'home' has a compound appoggiatura, and 'the' includes a trill which is also not typical of later editions or performances. The accompanying part is practical and unobtrusive.

Had this edition been a primary source of reference, it is conceivable that at least some of the later debates could have been avoided. It shows that from an early printing of the piece, there was a spirit of virtuosity to it that included embellishments, but that the accompaniment was simple (and which Ganz later notes is highly preferable). The *con spirito* marking and the presentation of a flute part suggest that the performance was approached in an upbeat manner, similar to other banner ballads. As such, it was not performed with the degree of silent reverence it is generally heard in the twentieth- and twenty-first centuries and which *The Code for the National Anthem of the United States of America*, published in 1942, sought to establish. As such, it is a mixture of constraint and relative freedom but certainly a piece that was to elicit a degree of energized emotion. Indeed, the original performance instructions suggest that if performed in this manner, a performance could be considered a violation of the Code's purpose.

The Early Discussions of a Standardized Version

In 1905, *The New York Times* published an article that said 'The Star-Spangled Banner' was:

> unsingable by a chorus of ordinary voices. When, at some public gathering, some misguided patriot undertakes to start it, the invariable result is a collapse in the middle of the first verse. Most of the singers forget the words; scarcely any of them can manage the tune.[11]

As Patrick Warfield[12] has shown, the discussion regarding a standardized version that Ganz would later continue began with a letter from Elsie M. Shawe, director of music in the St. Paul Public Schools, to President Theodore Roosevelt in October 1907. She argued for an 'authoritative version' of

Figure 2.1 The Star Spangled Banner, pub. Thomas Carr (1814).

The National Anthem and the Challenge of Standardization   41

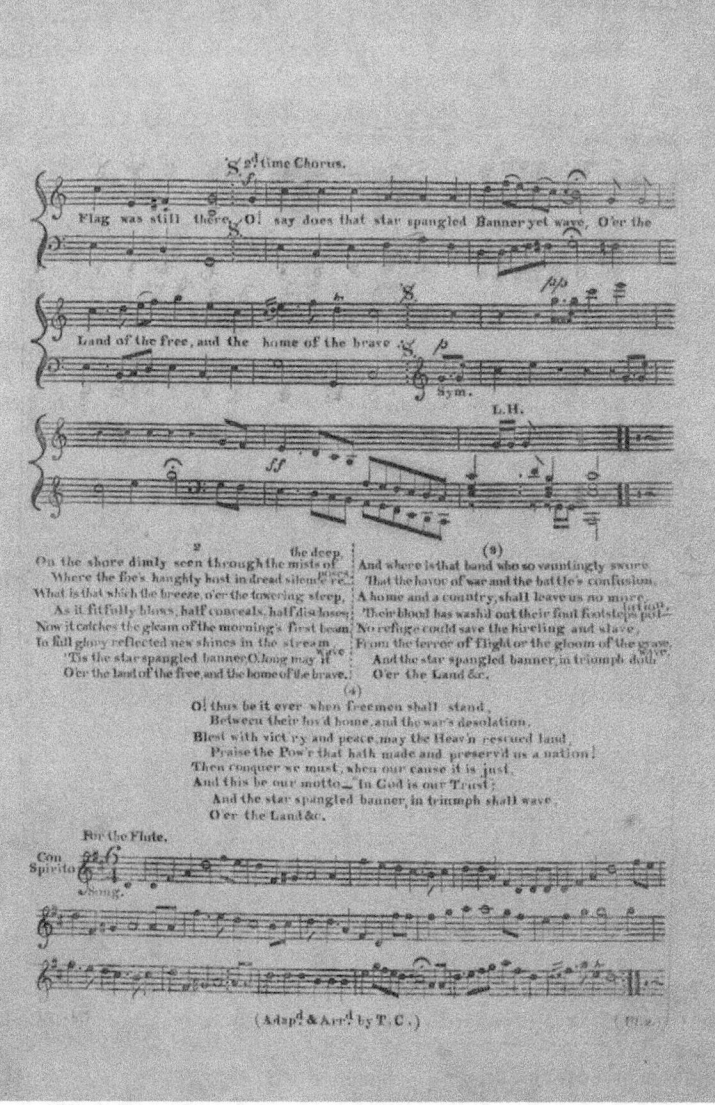

patriotic and national songs that could instill 'into the hearts and minds of the children a loyal love of Flag and Country'.[13] The letter was forwarded to the Librarian of Congress, Herbert Putnam, and then his assistant chief, Ainsworth Rand Spofford, and chief bibliographer, A. P. C. Griffin. As neither were musicians, they referred the matter to Elmer Ellsworth, Commissioner of Education, who suggested it was a topic for the Library of Congress, at which point Putnam sent it to the head of the music division, Oscar Sonneck.[14] In 1909, Sonneck published a report on 'The Star-Spangled Banner', 'Hail, Columbia', 'America', and 'Yankee Doodle'.[15] Meanwhile, in 1908, the National Education Associations' music division had formed a committee consisting of Elsie Shaw, Arnold Gantvoort, and Powell G. Fithian to work on a resolution for the 'Uniformity of National Songs'.[16] Gantvoort had already produced a version of the National Anthem that appeared in *The High School Ideal* (New York: American Book Company, 1897).

The concern of the NEA had been to provide a version that was consistent and accessible while being well aware that many versions were already in existence. One of these was in Sousa's *National, Patriotic and Typical Airs of All Lands,*[17] which, in addition to incorrectly attributing the tune of the 'Star-Spangled Banner' to Samuel Arnold,[18] removed the descending triadic opening, evened some dotted rhythms, and inserted awkward syncopations. In the orchestration, he maintained some of the writing from his earlier work, *The International Congress* (1876), complete with extensive scoring and embellishment. This is important to note because when Ganz and others were critical about 'German counterpoint' and overt embellishments, singling out Victor Herbert and Walter Damrosch at different points, the same critique was tempered with the popular American figure of Sousa. Although both Herbert and Damrosch were entrenched in American music-making, they were not born on American soil. Sousa was born in Washington D.C. and had joined the Marine Corps at thirteen and later directed the Marine Band in many successful recordings. There was an unimpeachable quality to Sousa's reputation, and yet, his version of the National Anthem was filled with the same problems of inconsistency that would plague committees in years to come. With so many different versions of the piece, including Sousa's being widely distributed, the NEA committee submitted a report in 1909 that noted that they had not been able to agree on a musical text.[19] However, a proposed version of the melody was submitted in 1910 and was discussed in meetings in 1911 and 1912. Gantvoort explained that in order to reach agreement, the dotted rhythms had been left out. This version was finally printed in 1912.[20]

A similar committee of the Music Supervisors' National Conference had also been working on a version under the leadership of Peter W. Dykema. The committee had studied how the anthem was currently being sung, noting the differences, and with a particular interest in how it was sung by the military, observing that there was a strong preference for using the dotted rhythms.[21] This was a marked contrast to the NEA version and a noted issue of inconsistency within the Sousa version. The dotted rhythms were sometimes associated with rag time, but the MSNC stated that 'whether or not this is connected with our liking for "rag time" may be a debatable question, but the tendency is certainly there. The NEA version, therefore, instead of simplifying the song by wiping out dotted eight and quarter notes, made it more difficult, because [it is] more foreign to our natural tendencies'.[22] The suggestion that the dotted rhythms were essential to the national identity and the absence of them was 'foreign' was a powerful statement, especially when directed at another professional body. Clague notes that 'the musical arrangement was rooted not in historical sources but in the way Americans realized Key's song in everyday life'[23] and the MSNC verdict draws on the same sentiment. This version became known as the Service Version, and three million copies were distributed at no cost to soldiers, most of whom did not read music. But the problem of standardization remained even within the military. Sousa's version was still used, and although the Service Music version was distributed, it was not standardized for broader use by any congressional resolution.

In 1914, the NEA forwarded their version to the Bureau of Education but there was no definitive response. The United States entered the war in April 1917, and at this point, the US Marine Band was still using Sousa's version. Eventually, the Bureau returned to the NEA resolution and organized another committee to review the matter, chaired by Will Earhart, director of music of the Pittsburgh Public Schools. The committee included Arthur Gantvoort, Oscar Sonneck, John Philip Sousa, and Walter Damrosch. As Warfield[24] has demonstrated by using the ballot of the committee (ca. October 2017) that showed their individual preferences, bar by bar, this was going to be a near impossible task to agree upon. Meanwhile, the War Department was now also looking for a version, and Damrosch and Gantvoort had scheduled concerts for the premiere of an approved version.

Sousa's response was the last to be received, at which point Earhart created a version that he felt best represented the various options suggested by the committee. However, with time running short before scheduled performances, there was a need for an agreed version. Damrosch was asked to use Sousa's 1890 publication as the basis of this version but instead created his own.[25] This was published without further review. What emerged was a reworking of a section of his *Manila Te Deum* (1898), and it was met with an especially poor reception. Gantvoort said 'it sure is "PUNK,"'[26] and music educators and publishers responded similarly.[27] The published vocal edition 'prepared at the request of the U.S. Bureau of Education' included the names of the committee and noted that it was harmonized by Damrosch. Beginning in unison, a second vocal line is added for 'and the rockets red glare' and then the two lower voices for 'O say does that'. Sonneck and Damrosch were greatly disappointed with the response, and John Alden Carpenter, a member of the Commission on Training Camp Activities, noted the 'futility'[28] of trying to find a solution that could be considered authentic.

The central question of whether an authorized version acknowledged by one institution could be accepted by another was not seriously entertained and consequently meant that, at the very least, two versions of the piece would continue to be used. Damrosch and Sousa each had their own versions, and their own interests in arranging performances of them. Matthew Mugmon has pointed out that 'Damrosch certainly had a personal stake in upholding the ideas of the song's value, as his own harmonization emerged the month after the Muck incident'.[29] By comparison, looking back to World War I, Sousa, considered by Warfield to be 'as much businessman as patriot',[30] observed that 'war could be simultaneously tragic and fruitful'[31] and Sousa had made considerable profits from his work. The March King's comments[32] had also become increasingly jingoistic and nationalistic as time had moved on although his relevancy was greatly diminished after the war had ended.[33]

However, the question that had been raised in Elsie M. Shawe's 1907 letter to Roosevelt remained unanswered. Indeed, far from gaining a consistency at a national level, there wasn't even a consistency between the different branches of the government. In 1942, the Service Version was printed with *The Code for the National Anthem of the United States of America*. This had been issued by the Music Educators National Conference following the work of their National Anthem Committee. The fact that a 'version' was published illustrates the problem of conformity, and the language of the Code also addressed this noting that 'it was inappropriate to make or use sophisticated "concert" versions of the National Anthem', while also observing that 'the slighting of note values in the playing or singing of the National Anthem will seriously impair the beauty and effectiveness of both the music and lyric'. These statements allowed for considerable interpretative scope depending on how they were to be understood, and in musical terms, the Code did little to clarify what was allowed. Despite this lack of clarity, the Code did state that 'Since the message of the music is greatly heightened by the text, it is of paramount importance that emphasis be placed upon the *singing* of the National Anthem'. This is an interesting statement because it suggests that the 'message', and thus emotion, engendered by the music has a definable role in the appreciation and value of the piece which, to some extent, can transcend the challenges of performance. As Clague comments, the 'expressive power'[34] of its flexibility is central to understanding the piece but standardization was increasingly far removed.

Despite the challenges, the performance of 'The Star-Spangled Banner' was now common practice. The St. Louis Symphony Orchestra (where Ganz would be appointed music director in 1921) played the anthem at every concert in November 1917, and Damrosch managed to turn the tide of criticism by regularly performing the piece. His 'impromptu' address to 3,000 children on February 3, 1917, the day the United States severed diplomatic ties with Germany, proved to be an extremely wise move, especially for an immigrant working in a public setting with an increasing hysteria about war in the press.

His reference to 'our' National Anthem, the country 'we love', his 'country of choice', and there being 'no dividing line' within the country where 'we are all citizens' was particularly well gauged and bears a strong resemblance to the texts of Ganz discussed in Chapter 1, especially *Music in the threatened areas*:

> One of the noblest functions of music is to arouse patriotism. Our National Anthem symbolizes to us the country we love, the United States of America. This comprises the North and the South, the East and the West. There is no dividing line. Whether we were born here or thousands of miles away, this is the country of our choice, and for which you and I must be ready at any moment to make any sacrifice. I want you, my young friends, to realize that what the flag symbolizes to the eye, the National Anthem symbolizes to the ear, and through the ear to the heart, demonstrating the great power of music to awaken our deepest emotions and to ennoble us in the awakening. We are proud of being citizens of New York, but we are still prouder of the fact that we are all citizens of the United States of America.[35]

Sousa, in his somewhat convoluted 1928 article about national airs in *The New York Times* that included a good deal of self-promotion, commented that:

> Perhaps we shall hear objections against a war song as the American National Anthem, but we have hardly reached that degree of human felicity where an anthem can be written without a strong emotional note ... an anthem must have emotion, and the emotion we understand best is love of our country.[36]

The House Judiciary Committee held hearings in January 1930 which unanimously approved the designation of 'The Star-Spangled Banner' as 'a method of further increasing the patriotism of the people of our country, and the continued popularity of the anthem'. This had been the sixth anthem bill (H. R. 14) proposed by Representative Linthicum (D-MD),[37] having begun his campaign in 1912. It was passed on April 21, 1930, without dissent. It passed the Senate on March 3, 1931.

However, music educators had voiced their concerns during this period regarding the text of the 'Star-Spangled Banner'. In March 1930, the Music Supervisors' National Conference passed a resolution opposing the adoption of 'The Star-Spangled Banner' as the National Anthem because it was a reflection of a single event related to war that did not represent the spirit of a nation. As Elizabeth Pontiff noted: 'reflected in this resolution [was] the understanding that music educators deeply affect the spiritual values of their communities and so must choose the music they teach with care and thoughtfulness.'[38] In 1945, Peter Dykema (MENC President, 1916–1917) felt that the most appropriate stanza to sing in a postwar environment, and with the recently founded United Nations, was the fourth stanza as it spoke of aspiration.[39]

Congressional Hearings

In early 1955, Representative Joel T. Broyhill (R-VA) became interested 'in urging the adoption of an official version of The Star-Spangled Banner' as a result of an inquiry by a group of high school students who requested copies of 'the exact words and music'.[40] Broyhill had previously introduced House Joint Resolution 341 on Flag Day, 1955, with the intention of a specific version being adopted. But in adopting the 1918 Education version which only had three of the four stanzas and didn't credit Key or Stafford Smith, it floundered. He tried again in 1957 having worked with the Library of Congress, bandleaders of the Defense Department, and thirty-six patriotic organizations.[41]

In a statement issued on January 9, 1963, almost five years after the 1958 congressional hearings on 'The Star-Spangled Banner', Broyhill summarized what he was trying to achieve:

> There is no document in existence containing the official, duly authorized or customarily used words and melody of The Star-Spangled Banner. Music stores sell an endless variety and composers continue to copyright new musical variations with little attention given to what words are used. The confused situation almost encourages changes. In too many cases changes are made for reasons entirely aside from the respect and reverence which should be paid to the historically famous poem and music.

This statement is wholly accurate because whereas the 71st Congress passed Public No. 823, signed by President Herbert Hoover on March 3, 1931, it was devoid of specific details:

> Be it enacted by the Senate and House of Representatives of the United States of America in Congress assembled. That the composition consisting of the words and music known as The Star-Spangled Banner is designated the National Anthem of the United States of America.

Broyhill introduced a resolution for the establishment of an official version and then notified the National Music Council, assuming that the forty-six music organizations that formed the Council would wish to voice their opinions. Dr. Howard Hanson served as president of the Council and he, in turn, appointed Mary Howe, William B. McBride (President of the Music Educators National Conference), Lieutenant A. R. Teta (Secretary-Treasurer of the U.S. Army, Navy and Air Force Bandsmen's Association), and Richard Hill, head of the music reference section of the Library of Congress who served as chairman.[42]

Hill noted how the issue of the initial copying of Key's words had set in motion a series of debates about the text alone:

> When the fourteen-year-old apprentice, Samuel Sands, took Francis Scott Key's manuscript in hand for the time to set the new poem in type, the broadside he produced introduced 43 changes from Key's manuscript. Admittedly, the changes primarily affect punctuation and grammar of the poem. Since the broadside, rather than the manuscript itself, was used as a basis for the first two newspaper publications of the poem, and since in their turn the newspaper publications spread the poem broadcast, Samuel Sands' alterations proliferated wildly.[43]

Although Ganz comments on the issues with inconsistencies with the text in his letters (below), his primary interest with the discussion that Broyhill had initiated rested with the music, both in terms of the melody and the harmonization of the melody. Ganz's personal marked-up copies of versions of the anthem, now housed at the Newberry Library, demonstrate the flaws he noted, principally poor harmony, voice leading, or 'German counterpoint' in the accompaniment. In a 1964 interview with the Chicago critic, Donal J. Henahan, Ganz commented that he would like the see the harmonization 'stabilized by law: 'Why should not the National Anthem be as sacred as the flag? No one would think of flying the flag sideways, or adding a star here and there, or revising the colors to suit himself. Why is it permissible to tinker with 'The Star-Spangled Banner?'.[44] 'It is not a question of whether you like the melody or not, either. It is the Anthem and everyone should sing as much of it as he can. If the French can sing the "Marseillaise" there is no such thing as an unsingable anthem. [Further] I was depressed at hearing one fellow conduct 'The Star-Spangled Banner' last season. So funereal. He probably didn't know the words or what they mean. The Anthem needs bite and excitement, the way John McCormack used to sing it.'[45]

As Hill had noted (above), there was no solitary source on which an authorized version of the melody could be based as numerous small changes had been made over time and gradually these had drifted into general usage. Alice T. Smith commented that 'perhaps it was the sincere emotion that accompanied the writing of the original that gave it an unquenchable spirit, an immortality that could withstand all controversy and competition',[46] but the degree of reverence that Ganz had long sought was taken up by Broyhill, and the spirit of competing versions was central to both of their concerns. To revert to an earlier authoritative version – Carr's 1814 edition was now very far removed from any of the versions in use – could also prove difficult to advocate for as both the musical text and performance style were in constant flux. As an example, it is only in 1843 that the descending triad that is associated with the first two words ('O say') appeared in print.[47] Hill noted that although the earlier committees worked independently, the versions they produced were, to him, remarkably similar:

> The pitch-line of their melodies is identical except for rhythmic differences [a point that exercised Ganz]. Since this same line has also been in most of the thoughtfully-prepared, modern versions, the present Committee sees no point in quarreling with it. The 'Education' version, which in general eschews dotted rhythms, used three quarter-notes on the similar melodic phrases (d, c, b-flat) to which the words 'proudly we' and 'ramparts we' are sung, although it dots the first of the notes when the phrase is sung to the words 'proof through the'. The Service Version dots the first note in all three instances.'[48]

Quite how these differences can be described in a vein that suggests they were minor is bewildering because clearly the piece does not sound the same with different rhythms, and this had been a major point of contention between the two earlier committees. However, this was the state of affairs that Broyhill encountered. I suggest that Broyhill and ultimately the judiciary committee were hindered from the outset because the interpretation that Hill provided did not suggest that the differences were of major consequence and had stalled the process of uniformity until that point. This was almost certainly unintentional as Hill was known for his assiduous approach to scholarship. Further, it was not shown that the challenges to consistency that began with Samuel Sands had already been reinforced and approved by different institutions or that different branches of the government were using different versions. Once the hearings began, they also showed the problematic nature of expert testimony, in this case by Hill, but later by Paul Taubman and Lucy Monroe.

Prior to the 1958 hearings, Broyhill received 5,000 letters from across the country that largely opposed any change. Chief among those complainants was Helen P. Lasell who had founded and ran the U.S. Flag Committee. In her *Be Alert Bulletin,* she argued that:

> all good patriotic minded people are satisfied completely with our NATIONAL ANTHEM as it is now – and as we have always known it – To tamper with it with the idea of changing or destroying it seems almost sacrilegious and certainly unnecessary and UN-AMERICAN.[49]

The initial response to the proposed bills was considered by a Subcommittee of the Committee of the Judiciary in the House of Representatives on May 21, 22, and 28, 1958.[50] Five bills (H. J. Res. 17, H. J. Res. 517, H. R. 10542, H. J. Res. 558, and H. R. 12231) and, in turn, five different options for review were considered. In his opening statement, the chair of the committee, Elijah Lewis Forrester (D-GA) remarked:

> MR. FORRESTER: Certainly this subcommittee approaches this hearing with reverence and affection. We realize that this is a responsibility we must assume and a decision we must make that will be in harmony with the heartbeats of all good Americans.

The statements that followed, many submitted in writing, involved not only marked differences of opinion but also significantly contrary approaches to the arguments. Early on the subject of which bill to consider as a superior version was confused still further by a statement from Elmer J. Holland (D-PA) who argued that a setting by Clarissa B. Nichol, a resident of Pittsburgh and a school teacher since 1914, should be adopted with the following argument:

> Statement of Hon. Elmer J. Holland [extract]: I think it is only fair that this committee take Mrs. Nichol's arrangement under consideration. The years that her copyright of this version have been in effect, the many schools using this version, and the money invested by Mrs. Nichol in her new book that is being published soon – all these points should be considered.[51]

Nichol's version was not seriously considered by the committee who instead began a discussion on the musical differences between the other proposals. However, the statement by Holland indicates the degree of personal support that members of the committee were prepared to invest in an individual from their own district. In an exchange between congressmen Whitener (D-NC), Forrester (D-GA), Zelenko (D-NY), and Drabkin (counsel), it soon became clear that none of them could read music. Zelenko commented:

> MR. ZELENKO: I think there is only one other bill that deals with the music. The others I think deal with the words, particularly, either having them remain the same or differences in spelling, or something like that ...
> [This was not the case but the chair responded ...]
> MR. FORRESTER: That question is answered.[52]

Broyhill's opening statement emphasized twice that he had no intention of changing or altering the National Anthem but only sought to address the:

> widespread misunderstanding which had come about since [he] first introduced a bill of this nature in June 14, 1955 (This was H. J. Res. 341 of the 84th Cong., which was then reintroduced on January 3, 1957, to become H. J. Res. 17 of the 85th Cong.).[53]

Broyhill sought to lay out the problems facing the committee as both the text and the music had inconsistencies in present publications. In what was to become an issue later in the hearings, he also raised the subject of the spelling of 'power' with or without capitalization of the first letter, a grammatical point that changed the meaning from one of strength to a reference to the Deity. Helen Lasell objected to using the lowercase 'p' on Power.[54] He explained how H. J. Res. 558 was based on the work of the National Music Council which had passed a motion on December 7, 1955, to appoint a committee to study the matter and had reached a conclusion that the musical and poetical text in Resolution 558 was the preferred version.

The need for standardization was likened to the need for flags to have the same proportions even if they were different sizes,[55] a point that Ganz later adopted.[56] Broyhill also explained that thirty-six patriotic organizations had been contacted for their opinion on the topic. He concluded by adding that he was 'not dogmatic [about his] support for House Joint Resolution 558 [noting that] If a suggestion for change should arise, [he] would be pleased to learn of it and to discuss it at length'.[57] In his comparison of the bills to aid the committee, his emphasis rested heavily on the issue of grammar, and it is clear that his understanding of the musical challenges, insofar as they were communicated to the committee in terms they would understand, was limited. In particular, he did not mention the issues of performance practice that occur because of inconsistent rhythms – a point stressed continuously by Ganz in his later correspondence (see Chapter 3) – or the considerable change to the melodic line that is suggested in Paul Taubman's version (see below) in H. R. 12231.[58]

During his exchange with Chairman Forrester, Broyhill proposed that he could play a recording of the music that was being considered in H. J. Res. 558 but this soon became a protracted practical matter:

MR. FORRESTER: ... [in agreeing to hear the recording] we are not going to have any Marine Band or anything of the kind, disturbing all of the offices all over Capitol Hill; that if we resorted to that, we would go to the river or some other auditorium where we wouldn't make a circus out of this hearing.

I do think it was the opinion, whether publicly expressed or not, that the subcommittee would have no objection to the playing of musical renditions, if it were by tape, and where it could be toned down and where the noise wouldn't invade the privacy of other people.[59]

After the recording was played, the discussion turned to the question of how an authorized version would be possible given the need for the anthem to be performed by different performing groups and Richard Hill, seated with Broyhill, commented that 'it would be extremely difficult to provide sufficient arrangements for all the different combinations of instruments' and that in terms of legislation the committee only needed to concentrate on the 'essence of the

The National Anthem and the Challenge of Standardization   51

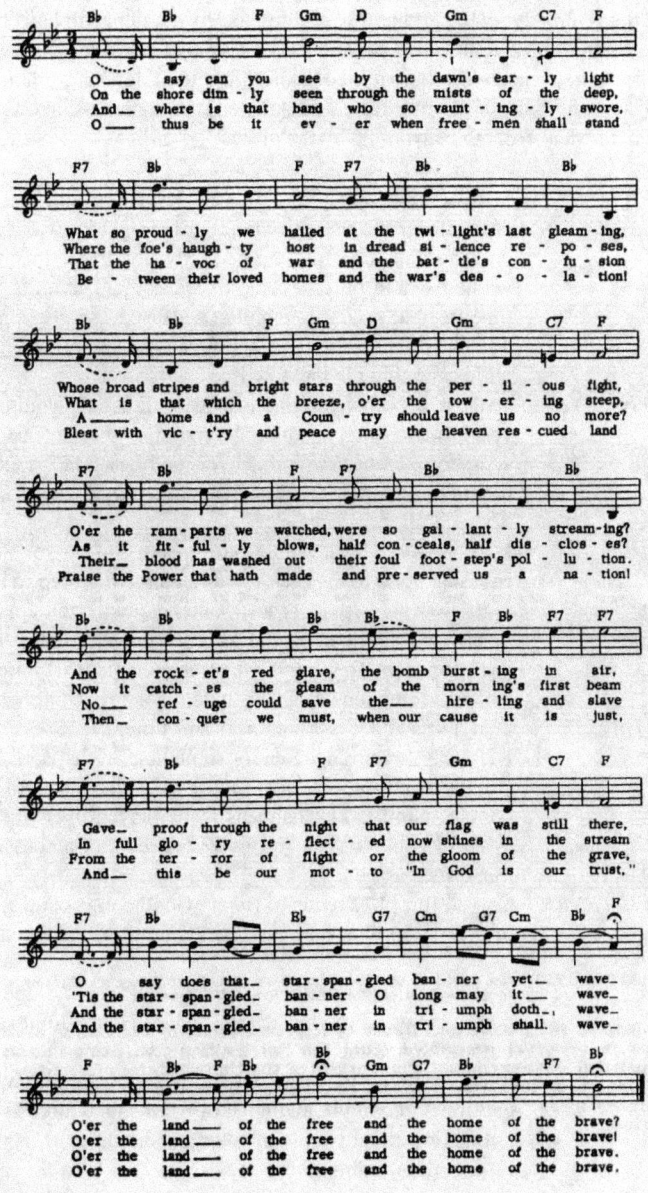

Figure 2.2 The Star-Spangled Banner – Proposed Official Version supported by the National Music Council (1958).

thing'.⁶⁰ Once again, putting the question of the accompaniment to one side and perhaps already realizing that it was going to be a challenge to have both the words and music approved by Congress, Hill continued with his answers but missed the critical point about the rhythm. Instead of agreeing grammar, melody, and rhythm, the committee was distracted with a discussion on how different musical ensembles would play the piece.

MR. HILL: ... we suggest that for different occasions some slight variation or the use of other chords in getting from one point to another would be perfectly possible. Since that version would only be used by one organization at one time it should cause no conflict because it is not going to be a question of disturbing the singers because the singers will be singing the melodic lines.⁶¹

MR. WHITENER: To have an official version for each situation would not you have to have an official version of the music for a symphony orchestra, another for the brass band, another for mixed chorus, another for male chorus, another for first-year piano-students?

MR. HILL: I do not see why it would be necessary to do so, sir. It could be done but we felt it was a dangerous step to take to try to provide this because somebody will try to play it on an accordion and they should be allowed to play it on the accordion. To ... provide arrangements [for] all possible combinations of voices would be more complicated than it seems necessary to be at this time.

Take a jazz arrangement or something of that sort. It is still the same piece to most people when they listen to any popular number that happens to be played over the air. When it is played, we recognize the roots of a composition quite easily.

MR. WHITENER: You do [but] I have heard Benny Goodman jazz up some of the old familiar tunes and they did not sound the same to me.

How will the uninitiated persons tell which is the official version of the music if we adopt House Joint resolution 558 and the Air Force Chorus will sing it, and the first-year piano player is playing it and a symphony orchestra is playing it, and none of them sound alike? I am not talking about you, I am talking about those of us with little musical training.

MR. HILL: ... We wanted to keep the basic elements of the piece the same without trying to hog-tie the entire country by making it always play exactly the same thing. That is, they have to play the same melody exactly and the melody is usually the thing that most people recognize a composition from. It is the most characteristic element. You would be surprised how much the harmonies can be varied without your even noticing it; unless you are a trained musician and know somebody slipped in a seventh chord, you would not even notice the difference, probably.[62]

Hill's answer does not acknowledge that in communal singing, a consistency of rhythm is essential for musical cohesion which, in the case of a National Anthem, is typically all the more necessary so that the performance, as well as the music and text, resembles a unified voice. In returning to the question of the 1931 legislation signed by Hoover, Chairman Forrester asks Broyhill if he knows whether the earlier committee that examined the legislation discussed whether they could resolve the conflict with the words or whether they did not wish to entertain the question of what Francis Scott Key had intended. Broyhill commented that the committee likely just accepted both versions as official to which Forrester responded:

MR. FORRESTER: I wonder if the committee was not confronted with the fact in 1931 that to be asked to resolve this conflict would be similar to being asked to rewrite the Ten Commandments[63]

Broyhill noted that there were currently 262 copyrighted versions of the 'Star-Spangled Banner' on file with the Library of Congress with numerous variations in the words. There wasn't even a consensus on whether it was a solitary bomb bursting in the air or bombs (plural).[64] He pointed out that this could cause confusion although that point was rebuffed by the chairman.[65] Later in the hearing, the subject of performance became briefly contentious, albeit with a rare moment of humor:

MR. WHITENER [TO MR. DORN]: Is it your idea that if we adopt an official version the FBI might go around seeing if folks are playing the official version?
MR. DORN: Of course not. Now I think you are being facetious.
MR. FORRESTER: Let's not have any argument.
MR. DORN: We are not arguing. ... We are old friends, Mr. Chairman.[66]

The point about performance is continually examined by the question of what it means to have a National Anthem that might be perceived as only performable by professional musicians when it is intended as a piece for everyone. This point casts aside Broyhill's previous analogy to the flag where it is assumed that someone stitching the flag would have the necessary skills to complete it and the knowledge of how to present the flag in public.

MR. FORRESTER:	Would there be any harm if the person playing the piano did not play it just exactly as you put it there [in the recording]?
MR. BROYHILL:	Would there be any harm if he changed it?
MR. FORRESTER:	A person playing the piano played it a little differently from what you set out there. ... What I am worried about is this. A lot of people play by ear.[67]
MR. BROYHILL:	You have me in a difficult spot when you ask me technical questions about music.
MR. FORRESTER:	We are in a difficult spot also. This matter has been thrown in our laps and we are going to have to try to decide.
	[Later in the Hearings Mr. Zelenko offered a similar comment.]
MR. ZELENKO:	I am just as much at a loss about that music as you are. I have to rely on expert testimony.

Once again, the committee has drifted into a tangential area. All pieces of music can be varied slightly but the question of whether there is an official version of the text and tune of a National Anthem is entirely different. If there is not an official version, then at what point does a degree of modification become unreasonable?

The atmosphere of doubt continued through the following minutes, occasionally referring back to issues regarding the text (owned by the Maryland Historical Society) and always stressing the importance of an official version to be considered. At a later point, the larger topic of consistency was almost derailed when the Chairman asked whether, as the National Music Council was affiliated with UNESCO, it was in turn also affiliated with Russia,[68] inferring that the NMC's version of the anthem could be viewed with suspicion or doubt.

Representative Dorn (R-NY) then spoke in favor of H. J. Res. 517 as it was set forth by the National Music Council. He cited Hill's text and noted that the difference between his version and Broyhill's was very minor and related to the capitalization of 'P' in 'power' (which H. J. Res. 17 did) and that it did not incorporate the third stanza. Mrs. William D. Leetch, secretary of the American Coalition of Patriotic Societies, criticized the fact that Hill had graduated from Oxford University commenting that 'This perhaps accounts for his purported concern lest the third stanza of our national anthem offend the British and so left it out'.[69] However, the questioning soon reverted to the issue of performance and the subject of legitimacy, with the topic of Russia already raised. Whitener advanced the suspicion by referring to the possibility of a 'clandestine' version being inadvertently sung by the military.

MR. WHITENER: ... Suppose that an orchestra plays what we might refer to as a "clandestine version" of The Star Spangled-Banner, assuming that we have adopted an official version. Are our military people and our laymen or nonmilitary people supposed to be able to distinguish between the clandestine version and the official version the Congress might adopt and remain seated [a breach of the Code] instead of standing if it is a clandestine version?[70]

In a subsequent questioning of a statement by Representative Zelenko, the topic of whether to use uppercase in 'Power' is discussed along with the possible history of the tune as a drinking song, a statement that has been proven misleading. As the anthem was already the official anthem of the country, it is unclear whether the diversion into the topic of drinking was ever going to have much bearing but meanwhile it proved a consistent sidebar reference that was one of the impediments to seeing passage of a bill with any measure of support. Again, there was intentional doubt about change and consequent standardization.

However, Representative Zelenko had an entirely different approach to the members of the committee, albeit with a strong, if problematic, argument. He incorporated the testimony of an 'expert witness', the singer Miss Lucy Monroe, and the composer, Deems Taylor. Zelenko stressed the need for everyone to be able to sing the National Anthem noting that:

> the average person goes about his citizenship in a most inarticulate way [with] his chores as a good citizen. How can he express himself? Very rarely does he get called upon to make a speech but when the Star-Spangled Banner comes along, he wants to sing it and shout it as loud as the next one. He finds he cannot do it. That is what I am trying to rectify.[71]

Figure 2.3 The Star-Spangled Banner, arr. Paul Taubman (ca. 1958).

The National Anthem and the Challenge of Standardization

He then continued to explain his rationale for supporting H. R. 12231, a version by the New York City-based composer, pianist, and organist, Paul Taubman. Zelenko stated that he wanted 'to be sure the man was a good American, too. I found out [that] he has a tremendous musical background, ... was a combat veteran of World War II and was decorated. That satisfies me'. What Zelenko failed to mention or perhaps didn't know was that Taubman was actually born in Canada, and so, if Taubman's version of the American National Anthem had been adopted, it would have been an English tune revised by a Canadian.

The following morning while the question of statehood for the US territory of Alaska was being discussed in the House, Miss. Monroe, a descendent of the fifth president, James Monroe, appeared before the committee. She described herself as someone who 'specialize[d] in singing The Star-Spangled Banner', having performed it over 5,000 times including for government functions and at international venues.[72] She commented that people wanted to be able to sing 'our song' (as Sousa, Damrosch, and Ganz had referred to 'our country')[73] but were unable to reach the high notes and that Mr. Taubman's revision should be adopted so they could. She added that she 'felt strongly that the basic melody should not be altered' and that the 'proposed version would make only the smallest changes, leaving the tune as beautiful and stirring as it has always been'.[74] If Zelenko understood the nature of this statement, then his comments to the committee were far from transparent because the changes that were proposed would have been unavoidably noticeable. Arguably, though the piece was out of the comfortable range for many singers, the most 'stirring' aspect of performance of the National Anthem is the inclusion of the phrases sung in a higher register, as Lichtenwanger observed.[75] Monroe's comments are interestingly juxtaposed with those of Enrico Caruso who, when asked about negative views on the anthem in 1917, responded 'Why, I will sing "The Star-Spangled Banner"; it's good enough music for me!' while noting that 'It ought to be good enough for those who make a living in this country'.[76]

The discussion following her opening statement immediately reverted to assessing the words and whether Monroe felt that these should be consistent, which she did. As Monroe was present as an expert on the musical aspects of the piece, her comments on the text might be seen as both less consequential and potentially distracting. She then referred to the musical changes proposed as enabling the less able singers to adopt a lower-pitched line to avoid high notes. However, the proposed version in the Resolution removes the higher phrases entirely, suggesting that they would not be part of the authorized version (see Figure 2.3).

Zelenko provided an extensive list of testimonies from the national press from people who confirmed that the higher notes were not possible to sing for the average singer. Later in his testimony, he read a statement from Deems Taylor who remarked:

> It seems to me that the fundamental qualification for a good National Anthem is that it can be sung by everybody. The Star-Spangled Banner in its present form cannot be sung by everybody. If we lower the key only the men are audible. If we raise the key only the women can reach the high notes. Mr. Taubman's proposal is excellent. ... To put the new version over, however, will not be easy for it will challenge a set of emotions, memories, and loyalties that have nothing to do with either the words or the music. Just the same, it should be done.[77]

Deems Taylor's comments about 'emotion, memories, and loyalties' are the very points that strike at the core of what would ultimately be a decision with political ramifications. A desire for consistency can also be portrayed as an attack on patriotism and individualism if misaligned. In Clague's opinion, in 2022, 'to standardize the anthem is to standardize patriotism itself'.[78]

Taubman's testimony began with an outline of his education and experience, not least as Musical Director of the National Broadcasting Company and Columbia Broadcasting System television departments. He made no mention of the fact that he was born in Canada but clarified that he served in the US Army from 1943 to 1946. He added that it was during his military service that he witnessed the challenges of singing the National Anthem.

> It was during my Army service that I became even more aware of the contention that I had held for many years, namely, the difficulty most people have in singing out national anthem, The Star-Spangled Banner. I observed that whenever a group of soldiers on march, or during a rest or recreational period raised their voices to any of the service songs or the popular songs of the day, they sand with great enthusiasm and abandon. However, when the occasion rose to sing our national anthem, just the reverse held true. Those men who happened to remember the words invariably would lower their voices, perhaps sing an octave lower, especially during the phrases that soar to the high register, or hum quietly to themselves. Others would remain mute, some just move their lips looking sheepishly ahead, while others would stop singing entirely after a few moments.

Of his changes to the original tune,[79] he remarked [the italicization is mine]. What I have done is *simply* the following: Beginning with the phrase "And the rockets red glare, the bombs bursting in air," I have *merely* lowered each note a minor third. Also in the phrase "O'er the land of the free," I have done the same thing, lowered each note a minor third.

I am sure the committee realizes that it is difficult to demonstrate a musical change without a musical instrument ... *I have in no manner, shape or form changed the rhythmic pattern or the melodic pattern of the melody as we presently sing it*...those professional singers and people of better than average voice who still elect to sing the high notes can very well do so and thereby add a rich harmony to the two most inspiring phrases of the anthem.[80]

Taubman then presented a recording with a singer, Stuart Foster, to demonstrate what his version entailed, and the two of them then discussed why the current version was difficult to sing. However, when they present Taubman's alternate phrases, only the individual phrase is heard and not in the context of the preceding and subsequent phrases. After further complaints about the original, they then performed the 'new version' in its entirety.[81] Quite how much of this demonstration the committee grasped is difficult to gauge but what was certainly not established is that the counterargument to Taubman's proposal is that he had suggested that only professional singers would likely sing the current version, whereas the overwhelming majority of the public would sing his revised version. Further, it is clear that no one on the committee would have understood the musical terminology regarding a musical line being lowered a minor third. Taubman's statement that he had 'in no manner, shape or form changed the rhythmic pattern or the melodic pattern of the melody' is a distraction because the rhythm was not the subject of his argument for a new version. Rather, it was the melody. He suggested that the 'melodic pattern' had not changed which only meant that the overall direction of the musical line remained intact. In fact, the very melody had been changed and quite significantly.

The remaining testimony largely circled around the same issues of text, grammar, and the difficulty of agreeing to the imprimatur of Congress for a specific version. The written testimony of many patriotic societies expressed the consistent view that they wished for an official version although the letters submitted to the committee often focused on one aspect of the issues at hand and seldom on the overarching challenge. However, near the end of the hearings, the committee heard from Daniel H. Burkhardt, Department Adjutant, American Legion, Department of Maryland, who began his remarks by reading a resolution that included the following text:

> Whereas under the plan of House Resolution 17 there is no safeguard to assure that some undesirable, Communist, subversive, or leftwing composer will not get the credit for a composition which might be adopted; and Whereas the many fine veteran and patriotic groups were not consulted

and invited to take part in any such consideration ...; Whereas we would not approve for one moment any place which might permit ASCAP to gain control over the playing of our National Anthem; ... we do vigorously oppose this resolution.[82]

Here, once again, was a Red Scare. Many groups had been asked for their opinions, as the hearings noted. But Burkhardt's comments touch on communism and from a man who had given numerous anti-communist speeches. More critically, they raised the subject of musical rights, which is an area the committee did not consider at length. Who would own the rights to any authorized tune? Representative Holland had observed this issue (above) in relation to Clarissa B. Nichol's version but otherwise it did not enter the hearings as a topic of discussion. If Taubman's version had been accepted and copyrighted by Taubman or his publisher, he would have been wealthy from the future profits of sheet music sales, rental fees, mechanical rights, and broadcast rights. It is in part for this reason that so many arrangements of other national anthems exist with compositions and arrangements by conductors who have the ability to select their own version for a broadcast. The question of 'who will benefit from our decision?' was not seriously raised by the committee.

Indeed, Taubman was unclear on where the issue would stand legally.

MR. DRABKIN: Either Congressman Zelenko or Mr. Taubman, could you tell me what the copyright situation is on this version?
MR. TAUBMAN: I still consider that the national anthem is P.D.
MR. ZELENKO: Tell them what that is.
MR. TAUBMAN: Public domain. My version could be called public domanic like any other arrangement. I certainly do not think there should be any monetary gain from the national anthem. The legal problem would have to be taken up. However, it would seem to me, sir, that it would still be public domain.

This argument is only partially compelling because although the tune would be considered public domain it does not satisfy the question of who would own the rights to the harmony of a given version. Taubman later states that he would 'love' for Congress to own the copyright of his version but it remains unclear which copyright they would be owning. His alternate melody or the harmony or the orchestrations?[83]

Near the end of the hearings, Richard Hill was recalled and asked to explain the history of the tune once more, so far as it was known, and also the origin of the words.[84] He remarked that during World War II, the Library of

Congress had received one or two dozen inquiries about the National Anthem in most weeks and now received possibly only one per month.[85] At the very end of the hearings, a discussion among committee members ensued regarding the publication of the testimony that had been offered because, in the words of Representative Nimtz (R-IN), 'it will contribute greatly to the ready availability of materials concerning The Star-Spangled Banner, its historical inception and its glorious history'.[86] For all his considerable efforts over three years, Broyhill's proposals had come to naught in terms of congressional legislation. This was in very large part because the committee did not fully understand what it was being asked about the National Anthem, and so many tangential topics were brought into debate. If the committee had first focused on agreeing the grammar of the text and then moved on to the rhythm of the tune or a potential adjustment of the melody, there would have been greater chance of success. But the environment was charged with self-interest, impatience, and relative insouciance by most members of the committee. Ganz kept a copy of the hearings in his file about the 'Star-Spangled Banner' and seven years later took up the matter himself referring to the work of the 1958 committee.

It can be argued that the discussion in the committee did indeed represent a national discourse. There was no overriding view or even a consensus between several members of the committee and the concerns raised were largely about points that were of interest to a particular member. The publication of the hearings does indeed provide a valuable document, but it is apparent that most, if not all, of the committee members had not studied the evidence presented in supporting documentation at any great length or considered that a discussion of the National Anthem should be continued or reach any conclusion. But it does provide an important window into the discussions of a musical topic in Congress during this period. Central to an understanding of the various rationales presented to the committee is the choice of expert witnesses. For these witnesses to be questioned by a congressional panel that was not musically literate initiates a dialogue that is fundamentally flawed. The issues at stake, whether of musical or literary text, were matters of important nuance to those who argued for them, but the importance of these points was almost wholly lost in the hearings. The broad language of Hill, as discussed above, and doubtless employed to simplify matters for the committee, only caused further consternation to the arguments when reviewed in context. However, this returns the debate to the central challenge, which is the lack of consistency that has, depending on opinion, either plagued the performance practice of the National Anthem or freed it from constraint. Independence of thought and practice had and indeed have prevailed in nearly all aspects of performance.

Notes

1. William Lichtenwanger, "Star-Spangled Bibliography," *College Music Symposium*, 12 (1972), 98.
2. Richard John Samuel Stevens, "Recollections," 1: 68, 70–73. Pendlebury Music. Library, Cambridge University. William Lichtenwanger, "The Music of 'The Star-Spangled Banner': Whence and Whither?," *College Music Symposium*, 18/2 (Fall, 1978), 54.
3. Lichtenwanger, "The Music of 'The Star-Spangled Banner'", 50–52.
4. Mark Clague, *O Say Can You Hear?* (New York: W. W. Norton, 2022), 39.
5. Ibid., 80, 81.
6. Ibid., 114.
7. "Maj. H. L. Higginson Defends Symphony," *Boston Globe*, November 1, 1917. Matthew Mugmon, "Patriotism, Art, and "The Star-Spangled Banner" in World War I: A New Look at the Karl Muck Episode," *Journal of Musicological Research*, 33 (2014), 4–26, 8.
8. Ibid., 8.
9. Bliss Perry, *The Life and Letters of Henry Lee Higginson* (Boston: The Atlantic Monthly Press, 1921), 485. Mugmon, "Patriotism, Art, and 'The Star-Spangled Banner,'" 8.
10. William Lichtenwanger, "Star-Spangled Banner. What Again?," *The Sonneck Society Newsletter*, 12/2 (Summer 1986), 59–51.
11. "The Star-Spangled Banner," *The New York Times*, March 24, 1905. Mugmon, "Patriotism, Art, and 'The Star-Spangled Banner,'" 21.
12. Patrick Warfield, "Educators in Search of an Anthem: Standardizing "The Star-Spangled Banner" During the First World War," *Journal of the Society for American Music*, 12/3 (2018), 268–316.
13. Shawe to Roosevelt, October 28, 1907, Record Group 12, Entry 6, Historical Files, File Class 900, Box 68, National Archives and Records Administration, College Park, MD. (RG 12, NARA II).
14. Warfield, "Educators in Search of an Anthem," 287.
15. This report was revised. Oscar George Sonneck and Library of Congress. Music Division. "The Star Spangled Banner" (Revised and Enlarged from the "Report" on the above and Other Airs, Issued in 1909) (Washington: Govt. print. off., 1914).
16. NEA, *Journal of Proceedings* (1908), 835.
17. John Philip Sousa, *National, Patriotic and Typical Airs of All Lands* (Philadelphia: Harry Coleman, 1890).
18. This was also a mistake that Ganz made as the front page of his own version demonstrates.
19. NEA, *Journal of Proceedings and Addresses of the Forty-Seventh Annual Meeting Held in Denver, Colorado, July 309, 1909* (Winona, MN: The Association, 1909), 673.
20. *Four Principal National Songs* (New York: American Book Company, 1912).
21. Elizabeth Pontiff, "MENC and the National Anthem; from the Early 1900s to Today's National Anthem," *Teaching Music*, 13/2 (October 2005).
22. *Music Supervisors' Journal*, November 1918, 4.
23. Clague, *O Say Can You Hear?*, 113.
24. Warfield, "Educators in Search of an Anthem," 268–316.
25. Clague, *O Say Can You Hear?*, 113.
26. Gantvoort to Earhart, December 18, 1917, RG 12, NARA II

27 Warfield, "Educators in Search of an Anthem," 300.
28 Carpenter to Engel, November 4, 1918, Engel Papers, Music Division, Library of Congress, Washington, D.C. Warfield, "Educators in Search of an Anthem," 306.
29 Mugmon, "Patriotism, Art, and 'The Star-Spangled Banner,'" 13.
30 Warfield, "Profitable Patriotism: John Philip Sousa and the Great War," *Over Here, Over There* (University of Illinois Press, 2019), 74.
31 Ibid., 75.
32 Ibid., 87.
33 Ibid., 92.
34 Clague, *O Say Can You Hear?*, 114.
35 Walter Damrosch, "One of the Noblest Functions," *Press and Sun-Bulletin* (Binghampton, NY), February 9, 1917, 3.
36 John Philip Sousa, "What Our National Anthem Should Be: In Both Sentiment and Music, Says," *The New York Times*, August 26, 1928, 69.
37 The tireless work of Linthicum is discussed in Ferris, 141–142, 157–161.
38 Pontiff, "MENC and the National Anthem."
39 Ibid., 18.
40 Joel T. Broyhill, Statement Concerning House Joint Resolution 4, January 9, 1963.
41 "The Star-Spangled Banner" Hearings before Subcommittee No. 4 of the Committee on the Judiciary, House of Representatives, May 21, 22, and 28, 1958 (Washington: US Government Printing Office), 21. Marc Ferris, *Star-Spangled Banner* (Baltimore: Johns Hopkins University Press, 2014), 188.
42 Richard S. Hill, "A Proposed Official Version of the Star Spangled Banner", *Notes*, 15/1 (1957), 33.
43 Ibid.
44 Donal J. Henahan, "Crimes Against Our Anthem," *Chicago Daily News*, July 5, 1964.
45 Ibid.
46 Alice T. Smith, "The Star Spangled-Banner," *Music Clubs Magazine*, 12.
47 Hill "A Proposed Official Version of the Star Spangled Banner," 34.
48 Ibid., 38.
49 *Be Alert Bulletin*, U. S. Flag Committee. January 10, 1958. Ferris, *Star-Spangled Banner*, 189.
50 "The Star-Spangled Banner" Hearings, 12.
51 Ibid., 14.
52 Ibid., 17.
53 Ibid., 18.
54 *Be Alert Bulletin*, U. S. Flag Committee. January 10, 1958. Ferris, *Star-Spangled Banner*, 190. Helen Lasell to George Radcliff, President, Maryland Historical Society, undated, typewritten letter. Cited manuscripts in Maryland Historical Society.
55 "The Star-Spangled Banner" Hearings, 20.
56 Rudolph Ganz, "The Star-Spangled Banner," *Music Clubs*, April 1965, 19.
57 "The Star-Spangled Banner" Hearings, 22.
58 Ibid., 26.
59 Ibid., 31.
60 Ibid., 33.
61 Ibid., 34.
62 Ibid., 34–35.
63 Ibid., 37.
64 Ibid., 36.
65 Ibid., 36.
66 Ibid., 50.

67 Ibid., 40, 77.
68 Ibid., 53.
69 Ibid., 127–142. Ferris, *Star-Spangled Banner*, 198–199.
70 "The Star-Spangled Banner" Hearings, 127–142.
71 Ibid., 60–61.
72 Ibid., 63.
73 Sousa, "What Our National Anthem Should Be," 69. Damrosch, "One of the Noblest Functions," 3. Ganz, *The Whitehouse*; *Is There an American School of Composers*; *Music in the Threatened Areas*.
74 "The Star-Spangled Banner" Hearings, 64.
75 Lichtenwanger, "Star-Spangled Banner," 59–51.
76 "Caruso Kisses Hand to America's Rocks," *New York World*, November 5, 1917. Mugmon, "Patriotism, Art, and 'The Star-Spangled Banner,'" 20.
77 "The Star-Spangled Banner" Hearings, 70.
78 Clague, *O Say Can You Hear?*, 114.
79 "The Star-Spangled Banner" Hearings, 73.
80 "The Star-Spangled Banner" Hearings, 74.
81 Ibid., 75.
82 Ibid., 145–146.
83 "The Star-Spangled Banner" Hearings, 78, 79
84 Ibid., 155–159.
85 Ibid., 160.
86 Ibid., 167.

3 The Advocacy of the Immigrant – Ganz and The Star-Spangled Banner

Ganz's involvement in the greater debate about standardization is significant because he used Broyhill's formal approach through a congressional hearing to energize and elevate his own correspondence with leading figures in American musical life. This allowed him to argue as both a musician and a patriot, and when considered alongside his own writings in Chapter 1, this demonstrates an especially public form of patriotism. Although many other immigrant pianists were known for their performances and arrangements of the National Anthem, not least Josef Hofmann, Vladimir Horowitz, and Sergei Rachmaninoff, none sought to pursue the issues of performance practice and stylistic integrity that Ganz did. Whether Ganz pursued this issue out of a spirit of awestruck patriotism that his visit to The White House engendered (as discussed in Chapter 1) or because he feared a backlash because of his European background, when he was often mistaken as German, is unknown. However, the sense of feeling 'threatened' as an immigrant was certainly present, as he noted in his comments about his naturalization in St. Louis.[1] It could easily have been a combination of both reasons. When he interacted with his students, he (carefully) described himself as both an American and a citizen of the world.

Stravinsky's controversial arrangement of the National Anthem and its very public patriotic gesture had, in his words, been made along similarly noble lines. He was also clear that it related to his naturalization. Stravinsky had finished the piece on July 1 but dated it as July 4, Independence Day. In his comprehensive study of the different versions by Stravinsky, Colin Slim[2] argued that one reason Stravinsky created his own version was also the lack of a standardized version, as well as the composer's own competitive sense.[3] In 1941, he wrote the following dedication to the American People, a different styling of which was also sent to President Roosevelt:

> Searching about for a vehicle through which I might best express my gratitude at the prospect of becoming an American citizen, I chose to harmonize and orchestrate as a national chorale the beautiful sacred anthem The Star Spangled Banner. It is a desire to do my bit in these grievous times toward fostering and preserving the spirit of patriotism in this country that inspired me to tender this my humble work to the American People.[4]

DOI: 10.4324/9781003430582-4

Clague comments that 'Stravinsky's *Banner* failed in its initial reception for more than one reason. Even if it had been a musical triumph, it would have been undercut by the increasing anti-Russian sentiments of the Cold War',[5] with the composer soon being accused of disrespect and subversive tendencies.[6] As Leonard M. Libbey later noted, 'Is nothing in America sacred to these iconoclastic foreign minds?' suggesting that the composer was guilty of 'some underhand and sinister motive'.[7]

However, for Ganz, it was a matter of the integrity and consistency of the score amid numerous published versions. In this respect, his advocacy for a standardized version was perhaps his truest patriotic commitment as an American because his concern was not simply with regard to the inconsistencies found in the melody and words but what he saw as the sacrilege of performance practice. Moreover, he did not seek to advance his agenda for personal profit, whereas Sousa and Damrosch certainly had an interest in self-promotion.

The issues, touched upon by Ganz in his correspondence, both contextualize and complement the 1958 committee hearings. In the following article, he takes up the charge that Broyhill had begun, noting the congressman's work and challenging the musical community to respond. Critically, he also uses language that, whether in jest or not, refers to a 'subversive' activity in relation to the bass line – the 'German counterpoint' – in some arrangements. This will not have been an accidental use of the word or a misunderstanding of its implication. Ganz's written English was extremely good. The timing, though, is important to note. The language and activities of subversion are inextricably linked with the House Committee on Un-American Activities, which was a standing committee from 1945 until 1975. Ganz's article was published in 1965, forty years after he had become a US citizen.

'The Star-Spangled Banner' [extract]

Dr. Rudolph Ganz

Music Clubs, **April 1965**[8]

Alice T. Smith's splendid story of "The Star-Spangled Banner" in the February issue of *Music Clubs Magazine* is an informative and lasting document in the history of our National Anthem. There is, also, an early story pertaining to the "Crimes against Our Anthem," an extensive and most cleverly written article by the well-known music critic of the *Chicago Daily News*, Donal J. Henahan, published in Chicago on July 4, 1964, and reprinted in many of the most important newspapers all over the country.

It was the outcome of an interview which Mr. Henahan had with me. For the last 45 years, I have conducted the Anthem with some of our leading symphony orchestras and for large audiences at the New York Stadium, the Hollywood Bowl, the Chicago Grant Park and some Spring Festivals, and played it in all of my piano recitals during the years of World War II, featuring a majestic but enthusiastic tempo (some of you may remember

John McCormack's unforgettably thrilling singing of "Oh, say can you see...") and a correct rhythmic enunciation of the melody, the tune of the song. The mistaken dynamic habit of a sudden change to *piano*, when the 'rockets' red glare, the bombs bursting in air' occurs, is quickly overcome with any symphonic organization when calling attention to the meaning of the words sung. As I well remember our audiences always sang these bars with patriotic fervor despite the unwarranted sudden soft accompaniment. Those who did not have the lowest or highest notes at their command omitted them but nothing seemed ever to be missing in the general singing.[9]

My collection of distorted versions, be it melodically, harmonically, rhythmically, or bass-ically, [referring to the bass line] is a shameful proof of the lack of respect from Francis Scott Key's inspired words to the then handy and popular song. If the French people can sing the not-at-all-easy "Marseillaise," then our nation should be able to master our "Star-Spangled Banner" in an impressive way and without hesitation. To me the flag and the anthem are ONE, on the same respected level. There are distinct rules about how the flag should be displayed. How about the return to the corrected initial melody and a simple accompaniment to the tune?

The FBI should have looked into the subversive activities in the bass and its strange harmonization of the well-meant patriotic version of the great and much-admired Igor Stravinsky, the rhythmical and harmonized errors in Walter Damrosch's much performed adaptation, the extremely busy version of our U.S. Army Band inclusive of the entrance of the notes of the first bars into the rocket and bombs area, the utterly objectionable counterpoint in Victor Herbert's 'South Fantasy,' the odd piano arrangement of the late great Josef Hofmann, unwisely extended upon by none other than the wonderfully gifted Van Cliburn, and finally, the explosive orchestra build-up by the revered Frederick Stock. What ethical, uncalled for errors in the presentation of a simple patriotic song. I have heard the flexibility of tempi of our anthem from funereal, pedestrian, too fast and hurried. Our government cannot and should not suggest a certain metronomic tempo. All that is needed is understanding, taste, respect, and fervor.

President Dwight D. Eisenhower wrote to Representative Broyhill about this situation on June 4, 1959 as following. 'I agree that an official version would be desirable, just as a standard pattern of stars in the flag itself is desirable. I would gladly sign a bill containing such a version'.

The bill has been supported by the National Music Council. How about our unique and immensely powerful National Federation of Music Clubs taking an active part in this needed effort to help Representative Broyhill to have our Congress adopt a version of our National Anthem with the original words and a simple accompaniment and thus make it a pure American expression?

The article draws on earlier narratives, not least the reference to Victor Herbert's version which Karl Muck had conducted.[10] The reference to the FBI was made in jest during the 1958 hearings when Representative Whitener had asked Representative Dorn, 'Is it your idea that if we adopt an official version the FBI might go around seeing if folks are playing the official version?'[11] Ganz, keen to be professionally diplomatic, is careful to speak well of Stravinsky, Van Cliburn, Stock, and Hofmann, with criticisms that are nonetheless veiled in respect and parallel compliments.

Ganz also noted in an interview with Henahan that the Stravinsky version of 1941 was booed when Hans Kindler introduced it to a Baltimore audience even though it was performed in wartime. Stravinsky later withdrew it.[12]

Broyhill continued to try and get a bill passed for another fifteen years, and during this time, Ganz referred to Broyhill's work while trying to garner support in the musical world with senior colleagues. The following letters to Howard Hanson, then Dean of the Eastman School of Music, and Hans Heinsheimer at the publisher's G. Schirmer, lay out the concerns and contextualize the Henahan interview (above) which was soon to take place.

Letter to Dr. Howard Hanson [extract]

June 15, 1964

> It is too bad and terribly selfish on my part to bother you at this time with what I call an <u>emergency</u> situation which I thought could be solved without your help and influence. No! I am to have an important interview with the music critic of the Chicago Daily News, Donal Henahan. The resulting article is to appear within the next two weeks. Subject: The National Anthem, its distortions and its different, undignified and overloaded orchestral settings. I have been in touch with Edwin Hughes, Representative Broyhill and Lt Colonel Curry of the U. S. Army. Fred Stock's cymbal and gran casa on ever second beat, Walter Damrosch's German counterpoint and now the Army Band with its canon.
>
> It is unethical, unfair and decidedly alarming. Who in Europe would dare to have such indecent fun with an Anthem[?] Do you own or will you make a final simple, undisturbed orchestra and band setting? Our nation is used to sing[ing] the Anthem as simply as it is now shown in Repr. Broyhill's resolution. So let us have an unadulterated accompaniment and have it accepted by Congress.

Letter from Howard Hanson, Eastman School of Music [extract]

August 3, 1964

> I agree wholeheartedly with your concern about our National Anthem. It should be possible to write a simple, direct and 'non-eccentric' setting of our anthem. The problem, I am sure, would be getting any action from the Congress on any arrangement!

In any case let me think it over and see what I can do. [Ganz adds a hand-written "?" at this point and circles the sentence]

Hanson does not commit to writing the setting himself nor does he suggest that anyone else compose it either. It is this vagueness that is compounded by the last sentence above that appears to challenge Ganz's patience. The tone from Hanson is at once friendly but professionally astute. If Hanson had made an arrangement that was adopted, then, by default, the issues of rhythmic inconsistency that had plagued the different versions since Sousa's published edition[13] in 1890 would have been resolved. As such, Ganz was trying to solve the argument by other means. The suggestion in his article, 'The Star-Spangled Banner',[14] that the National Federation of Music Clubs back a particular version was another route toward the same potential outcome.

Letter to H. W. Heinsheimer [G. Schirmer, Inc.]
July 26, 1964

This is a rather important letter as far as I am concerned. The enclosure [presumably the newspaper article of Henahan referred to above] speaks for itself. Unfortunately, Mr. Henahan failed to mention your Damrosch edition of the National Anthem which we discussed thoroughly during my interview. In a way, I am glad of it. This orchestration is well made except for the unpardonable 'German' counterpoint in bars 5 (the rhythm is incorrect), 6, 7, 9, 10, 11, 12, 14, 16, 17, 18, 19. The upbeat to the Anthem is not [beamed separately] but [beamed together]. I wish that Schirmer could publish a simple version which would settle the entire matter. I am sure Congress would make it official. Please let me have your reaction.

In old friendship and loyalty to your great firm, I am

Most cordially,

Rudolph Ganz

The reference to 'German' counterpoint is highly, and arguably intentionally, misleading and provoking and recalls the Karl Muck story discussed in Chapter 1, both because of the issues of Muck's misunderstood situation and the Victor Herbert version that he was known to conduct. To a musician, 'German' counterpoint infers a second truly independent line to the melodic line that potentially has its own character. What Ganz is actually referring to are passing notes or a 'walking bass' that create harmonies he considers unnecessary. It is this (nonessential) melodic activity within the harmonic framework that irritates Ganz in addition to harmonies that some composers have allied with the melody to begin with. However, the harmonies, like the rhythmic inconsistencies, were not a prominent concern to the 1958 committee. As the committee could not agree on a rhythm, the possibility for consideration of the harmonies (or counterpoint) that Ganz is concerned with would have been even more remote. Hill's reference to the 'traditional chord progressions of the 19th century' in the following commentary on the committee's work was also problematic because of the question of whether a prevailing harmony heard with a unison rhythm is to be considered the same as one where, in a typical four-part texture, the bass line can be more active:

> As for the harmony, there seems to be no question that this should employ the traditional chord progressions of the 19th century. A piano harmonization, however, generally calls for the use of block chords most of the time, whereas editions for string quartet, orchestra, and band will require more counterpoint. On occasion, the counterpoint may be fairly elaborate without producing perceptible dissonance. Since an 'official version' cannot help but exercise some restrictive effect, it seems unwise to provide even so much as a specific bass-line, lest there be those who might suppose that all basses for the anthem must follow this exact line. Thus chord symbols have been suggested above the melody line, but no actual working out of the accompaniment has been provided.[15]
>
> Finally, it was felt that certain interpretations should be clearly stated, partly to minimize the restrictive elements inherent in any "official version", and partly to clarify certain attitudes and problems which could not very well be covered in the version itself.
>
> The purpose should be made sufficiently clear by a reading of the Commentary.

[The commentary included the following statements.]

> A traditional series of chords has been given as a guide toward a suitable accompaniment for the melody. Although strange and bizarre harmonizations should certainly be avoided, it is recognized that reasonable latitude must be allowed.
>
> The anthem should always be performed in a manner that gives it due honor and respect. It should never be performed as part of a medley or in circumstances where its importance as a national symbol is any way cheapened.

Arguably, Hill's approach to the musical language of the piece did not help the committee or the decades-old discussion and the suggestion that providing a bass line could be some sort of impediment, despite the commonly understood practice of harmony being derived from bass notes (particularly for a piece as harmonically straight forward as the National Anthem) is perplexing. There is also no clarification on what would constitute 'bizarre harmonizations' or what degree of latitude would constitute a performance that 'cheapened' the reception of the piece. Whereas Taubman's comments[16] in the hearings were carefully gauged to avoid controversy, Hill's explanations are fraught with vague suggestions delivered as fact. As a letter from Harold Spivacke notes, Hill's views were also not the official position of the Library of Congress either.

Letter from Harold Spivacke, Chief, Music Division, The Library of Congress [extract]

July 27, 1964

> As you doubtless know, the matter of an official version of the National Anthem was a matter of deep concern to the late Richard S. Hill,[17] former head of the Reference Section of this Division. Mr. Hill served as chairman of a National Music Council committee to devise an acceptable official version, and the National Music Council version was incorporated in several bills, the most recent of which was introduced by Mr. Joel T. Broyhill of Virginia during the 88th Congress.
>
> Of course, we have hundreds of versions of the 'Star Spangled Banner' in the Music Division. However, Mr. Hill's solution to the problem, as approved by the National Music Council, appears to me the simplest and most satisfactory one. I need to say that this should not be taken as an official position of the Music Division. Rather, it represents the thoughts of Richard S. Hill, one of its most distinguished scholars who devoted much time and energy to restoring the original.

As discussed in Chapter 2, the NMC version (referred to by Hill, Figure 2.2) does indeed resolve some of the issues that Broyhill was addressing but Hill's comments about harmony, counterpoint, and nineteenth-century practice were confusing from a musical perspective and beyond the understanding of the 1958 congressional committee.

A reply (7/28/64) from Heinsheimer to Ganz addresses the point that Deems Taylor had made in the hearings regarding the 'emotions, memories, and loyalties'[18] that people associate with the National Anthem. The general public was very familiar with the Damrosch version, and thus, the challenge of whether any modifications to melody, rhythm, or text would actually be adhered to in public performances was debatable.

Letter from H. W. Heinsheimer, G. Schirmer, Inc [extract]

July 28, 1964

> The feeling here is that Schirmers are so closely associated with the Damrosch Orchestration for Orchestra and the Damrosch-Sousa Setting for Band that we should not issue another orchestration of the National Anthem.

Below the signature is a handwritten annotation of Ganz. An identical text appears in a handwritten note on Chicago Musical College letterhead bearing the date 8/2/64. Ganz was sending copies of the NMC version that Broyhill had promoted to colleagues as he tried to further his cause:

8/2

Enclosed please find the version of the N. A. as suggested by the N. M. C. and as offered for adoption by Congress by Representative Broyhill. Don't you think it would be advisable to have a corrected version printed, eliminating the rhythmical distortions, the softened "rockets" and "bombs" and the wrong harmonization at least[?]

Sincerely yrs,

R.G.

Ganz was also in touch with Edwin Hughes of the National Music Council, as the letter to Hanson (June 16, 1964) notes. By November of the same year, Ganz had moved the discussion forward by suggesting that if the American Symphony Orchestra Association were to adopt a single version for its members to perform, then definitive progress would be made. Once again, Ganz decided to work through institutional bodies while no progress was being made in Congress. However, the suggestion in the subsequent reply that the harmonies be approached 'in the usual way,' presumably referring to Damrosch, would not have been welcomed by Ganz.

Letter to Dr. Edwin Hughes [extract]
November 12, 1964

Is the resolution still alive and has Howard Hanson followed my request to write a simple harmonization of our dear anthem?
The most powerful help we can get is from Mrs. Thompson, president of the American Symphony Orchestra Association. If we ever have a version compatible with Broyhill's melody and a simple harmonization, Mrs. Thompson is the one who could propose to her board to oblige all members of her gib [good?] organization to abide by this definitive version.

Letter from Edwin Hughes, National Music Council
November 17, 1964

Dear Rudolph,

Thank you for your letter of November 12, and for your contribution [dues] to the National Music Council and the newspaper clipping, which shows that you are still on the trail of a solution to the adoption of an official version of the words and music to the 'Star-Spangled Banner'.

We received no news during the last session of Congress that Mr. Broyhill's bill was re-introduced. Perhaps he will be considering this when the new session meets. I think that any further action on his part will probably hinge on whether or not he gets a lot of letters from persons who are interested in having the National Music Council version adopted as the official one.

Howard Hanson has not told me about your request to write a harmonization of the anthem. It was decided by our Committee on the Star-Spangled Banner to print the melody and simply to indicate the harmonies in the usual way, leaving some leeway for utilization of the melody by different groups, instrumental and choral.

With warm greetings and regards,

Sincerely yours,

Edwin Hughes

Letter to Edwin Hughes [extract]
January 6, 1965

The Secretary of the NFMC [National Federation of Music Clubs] has asked me to write an article about the 'Star Spangled Banner'... It deals with the anthem from its birth to the "resolution" of Representative Broyhill. ... So I am to write a new effort. My new effort is to achieve what is due to our 'Star Spangled Banner'.

Miss Winterberg, upon my request, has written Howard Hanson for that simple harmonization which I am sure we all would like to see realized. To indicate the harmonies is not sufficient. I will criticize severely the unfortunate Damrosch version which is in error melodically, rhythmically, harmonically, and stylistically. (The piano ((*p*)) approach to rockets and bombs.) Do you think that it would be improper for me to make the simple harmonization for that April issue, if Howard or you or anybody equally competent will not do it[?] So, after April I shall put the mute on my patriotic efforts.

Letter from Edwin Hughes, National Music Council
[extract]
January 13, 1965

I hope that you will hear from Howard Hanson in regard to making a simple harmonization of the anthem. As you know, Howard is very busy with lectures and conducting engagements in various parts of the country and with his new work at the University of Rochester.

[There is no mention of Ganz's offer to write the harmonization himself.]

The Ganz Version of the National Anthem

There are no records of Howard Hanson completing a setting of the National Anthem as Ganz had suggested. However, among the Ganz papers at the Newberry Library is a manuscript that shows Ganz's intentions with regard to both the rhythm and the underlying harmony. Ganz's preference was clearly for a simple unadulterated version although the difficulty with presenting something that is seemingly straightforward is that it can be embellished in performance or indeed in publication unless that is actually forbidden.

As noted in Chapter 1, the Thomas Carr version of 1814 had both a simple accompaniment and a vocal line that suggested a degree of virtuosity with trills and a compound appoggiatura. Further, the nature of convincing embellishments can easily be seen in the reharmonization of Christmas carols, especially the final stanzas replete with descants. Interestingly, the question of descants to be sung above the melody is seldom, if ever, discussed with regard to national anthems. In the case of the 'Star-Spangled Banner', this would also be near impossible to successfully accomplish because of the already broad range of the melody line. The solitary exception to this would be the 'crowning' of the last note of the penultimate phrase on the word 'free', whereby the tonic note is often heard in performance (after a brief pause), a fourth higher than the note of the tune. This tradition appears to have started with Josef Hofmann's piano version of the piece, and stylistically, it is a mirror to his lower octave rhythmic punctuations (on the second beat of the bar) for the rest of the arrangement. That an embellishment occurs on the word 'free' is naturally a pleasing coincidence for those who view the anthem as a piece that has an individual aspect to performance.

History has a tendency to work out the rough edges of arguments and let prevailing practices prevail. Ganz's approach (see Figure 3.1) and thoughts about the overarching debate proved correct as there are presently three common 'versions'. The first and most well-known orchestral version remains the Damrosch setting with all of the 'German counterpoint' that drove Ganz to distraction. Meanwhile, a succession of American hymnal editors have included the National Anthem alongside other patriotic hymns in their published volumes across several denominations. These are uniformly musically conservative which is interesting in itself because liturgy allows for descants and reharmonizations as a standard practice in many congregations.[19] However, when it concerns the National Anthem, which is rarely sung in churches, the hymnal editors have consistently opted for unobtrusive versions and also included only one or two stanzas out of the possible four. The third performance practice is the one that Ganz and Broyhill most feared because it involves the ready embellishment of the melodic line by performers. For Ganz, it would have seemed outrageous for an untrained singer to perform the National Anthem at a significant public event and a complete affront if a singer then changed the melody and personalized it. In my own experience, I can recall attending a university commencement ceremony where a singer routinely changed the basic melodic line, added rests, took breaths between words where there was no grammatical punctuation, and generally turned the performance into a highly individual interpretation. Embellishments have become the norm rather than rare occurrences. The version (Figure 2.2) proposed by the committee led by Hill sought to provide not only an authorized text but a regularized rhythm so that each line begins with a dotted eighth note rhythm but then has a simple subdivision later in the line. The harmony in the NMC's version does not deal with the question of chord inversions, and so, there is no guarantee that, though the harmony could indeed be consistent, it would necessarily be elegantly interpreted. The NMC's version could sound accurate but perfunctory.

When looking at Ganz's larger argument for as much to be agreed officially as possible with respect to text and music, time has marched on, and the point of strenuous debate has very largely passed. Bearing in mind the challenges of work across several decades, beginning with the response to Elsie M. Shawe's letter to President Roosevelt in 1907, and the prevailing vagueness of the 1958 committee's deliberations, this is unsurprising as traditions tend to follow the path of least resistance, and no consistent guidelines were put in place. However, when people chide performers in our own time and ask how it can be that a soap opera star is allowed to musically brutalize the National Anthem, the answer cannot be because concerns were not raised at the highest level before. To quote President Eisenhower in 1959, 'I agree that an official version would be desirable, just as a standard pattern of stars in the flag itself is desirable. I would gladly sign a bill containing such a version'.[20]

On February 19, 1965, Ganz received a letter from Sidney R. Yates, Member of Congress for the 9th District, Illinois, congratulating him on receiving The Order of Lincoln noting 'It couldn't be more highly deserved and I think it's most appropriate that you should be the recipient of the Academy's first award'.[21] Gates wrote again two years later to congratulate Ganz on his ninetieth birthday acknowledging him as 'Chicago's Ambassador of Music to the World' and observing the 'wonderful contribution [he had] made to the American people'.[22]

Ganz died on August 2, 1972, and his personal campaign for a standardized version did not come to fruition. However, the Ganz Papers at the Newberry Library include not only his markings of faults found in other editions but also the autograph of his own version (see Figure 3.1). The 'original' music and text appear on the top line.

Advocacy of the Immigrant – Ganz & Star-Spangled Banner 77

Figure 3.1 The Star-Spangled Banner, arr. Rudolph Ganz (ca. 1965).

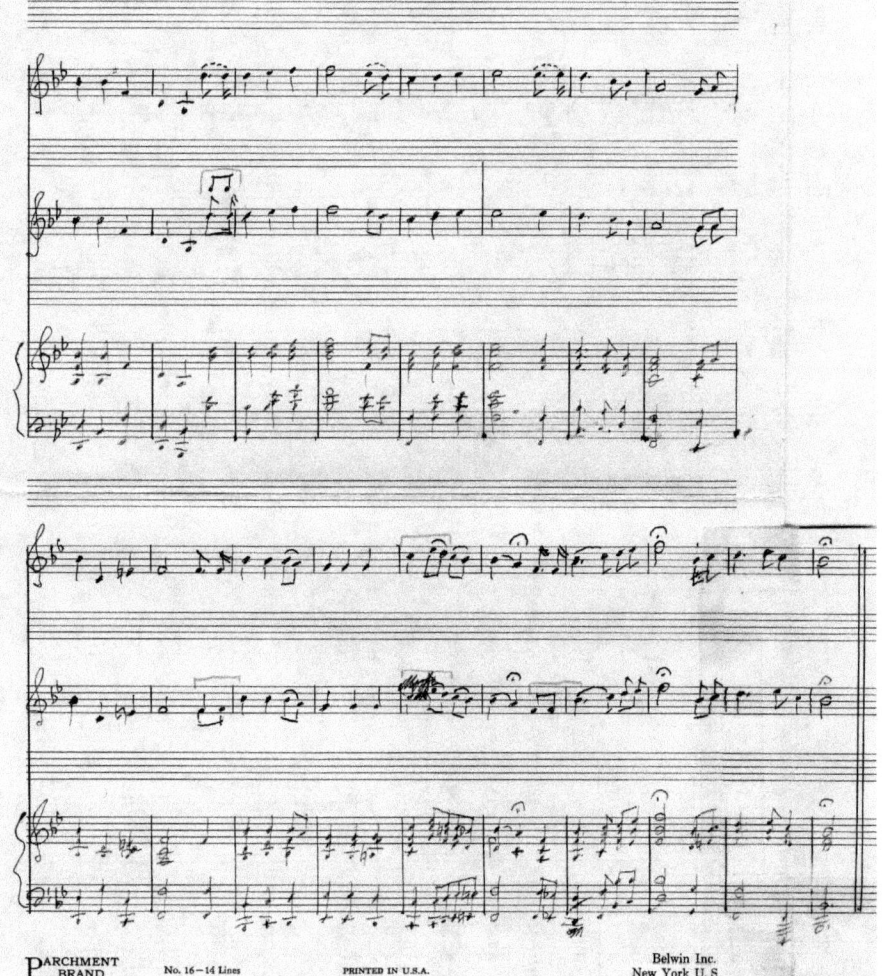

Ganz corrected the beaming of the initial anacrusis in order that there are upward and downward stems to reflect the difference in the number of syllables in each stanza. His principal concern was with dotted rhythms, which he marks with red brackets, and these he evens out so that the dotted rhythm of the anacrusis is mirrored in the upbeat to the third bar ('by the dawn's early light'). This is then balanced by even eighth notes starting the phrase at the end of bar four ('what so proudly we hailed'). In the second section, beginning at the end of bar 16 ('And the rocket's red glare'), he appears to self-correct himself so that there are no more dotted eighth notes for the remainder of the piece including the end of bar 24 (which on the second stanza would begin "'Tis the star-spangled banner'). The same is the case for the end of bar 28 ('O'er the land') which becomes equal eighth notes as does the beginning of the very last phrase ('and the home'). The accompanying harmony is devoid of anything that could be regarded as an embellishment.

Broyhill's interest in a standardized version began in 1955. Following the 1958 hearings, he tried again with another bill in 1962, having already gained support from President Eisenhower in 1959. The 1962 bill included all four stanzas, but Helen Lasell was ready once more and, having studied the 1931 law that had made the 'Star-Spangled Banner' the official National Anthem, she concluded that the version the House Judiciary Committee had heard played in 1930 was already an official version. She then attacked Broyhill's bill and wrote about people 'who constantly strive to destroy our heritage and all we have cherished'.[23] Despite sponsoring a March 1962 concert at Constitution Hall, Washington D.C., featuring the U.S. Army Band, Broyhill was behind in the public relations disaster that was unfolding.[24] But he did not stop his own campaign, and on January 3, 1973 put forward H. J. Res. 26 – A resolution to adopt a specific version of the Star-Spangled Banner as the National Anthem of the United States of America. In total, he had introduced nine bills about the National Anthem. The timing of the final resolution could not have been worse for a topic that had a potentially critical political outcome, and Broyhill was also nearing the end of his career.

On June 17, 1972, the offices of the Democratic National Committee had been broken into in the Watergate building. By September, Howard Hunt and Gordon Liddy had been indicted. Although President Nixon was re-elected on November 7, *The Washington Post* had been reporting developments relentlessly since three days after the Watergate break in. The unsettled environment this provoked was compounded by the loss of Hale Boggs. The member of the US House of Representatives from Louisiana's Second District from 1947, he served on the Warren Commission, and in 1971 became House Majority Leader. On October 16, 1972, he was onboard a twin-engine Cessna 310 with Representative Nick Begich of Alaska when the plane disappeared between Anchorage and Juneau. On November 24, the search for the passengers was suspended, and the remains of the passengers and the plane have never been found. It was the third flight Boggs had taken in relation to the visit to Alaska that day. He traveled first from Texas to Washington and then to Anchorage. He was driven to the Texas airport by a Yale law student who would become the 42nd US President, William Jefferson Clinton.

On January 3, 1973, with Tip O'Neill as House Majority Leader, House Resolution 1 officially recognized Bogg's presumed death. Broyhill's resolution regarding the National Anthem was referred to the House Judiciary Committee but not brought forward for further discussion. Broyhill left the House in 1974, and the question of an official standardized version of the National Anthem has not been raised since at a congressional level. However, in 2005, the National Anthem Project began a three-year term to promote singing of the National Anthem with First Lady Laura Bush serving as the honorary Chair and with support from Jeep, Chrysler, Save America's Treasures, the Girl Scouts of America, the National Basketball Association, the U.S. Conference of Mayors, the National Education Association, and the American Legion. The need for the project was supported by a recent Harris poll that showed that fewer than 30 percent of American children were able to sing the piece. Representative Ted Poe (R-TX) commented on the floor of the House that:

> Now, in many American classrooms they do not start American history with the American revolution [but] with World War II [and] so how can we blame our young children who become our young leaders if they do not know our history.[25]

While the project aimed to promote singing of the anthem and achieved great advances in many places, the focus was not on an authorized text, tune, rhythm, or harmonization. These points remain unresolved.

With the increasing embellishments added to the anthem by guest singers at sporting events, Hill's arguments regarding a necessary flexibility have been taken to a far greater extreme than any of the earlier committees could have imagined. For Ganz, it would have been incomprehensible to sing the National Anthem with such a wide array of liberties in performance but the argument for relative individualism in performance styles and indeed accuracy of basic pitches in some cases has overtaken what Congress had seriously considered to be a need for discussing a standardized version. It is fair to suggest that the problem came from the considerable number of early versions which set in motion a perpetual debate. As the nation has evolved with a free and independent spirit so too has emerged an anthem than an individual can call their own, and the discussions and debates can also be seen as imbuing a democratic spirit, indeed an especially free spirit. But these historic discussions also shed light on the nature of discourse about a topic that is as charged with emotions and political ramifications as the National Anthem.

As shown in Chapter 2, the 1958 hearings discussed the topic of subversion and Ganz was not beyond using carefully chosen language about subversion and the war to further his own patriotic arguments and reputation. Given the nature of wartime hysteria and the need to assert unequivocal patriotism and, furthermore, to do so publicly, he was wise to take this approach. Across several decades, Ganz shows how, as an immigrant, he was able to navigate a diplomatic route that several others failed to find. His comments demonstrate how he positioned himself as representing the finest qualities of the Old World while promoting American culture and an expected patriotism, not least through a deep devotion to seeking a standardized version of the National Anthem. But there remains a lingering question of why Ganz felt compelled to devote so much time to this discussion in an already busy life. In placing the correspondence of Ganz alongside his respondents in the context of the unsettling circumstances many immigrant musicians faced, I am left with the conclusion that Ganz did not pursue this matter simply for musical reasons and wisely stayed clear of any impression his interest was political attention either. Rather, Ganz's experience and involvement mirrors the larger picture of the relationship between American politics and culture for which the National Anthem is a natural beacon of attention and potential controversy. Debates and discussions within the confined environment of professional organizations and between professional colleagues do not fare well when they enter a committee room of Congress, as the 1958 hearings demonstrate. The discussions frequently veered off the central topic and were mired in misunderstandings, points of confusion, and a bias of information presented.

In 2023, it seems near impossible to imagine a similar congressional committee with members of opposing parties discussing a topic as potentially controversial as the performance of the National Anthem and executing this responsibility with the same consistent tenor of approach found in the 1958 hearings, which was often quite humorous. The relative diplomacy of the 1958 hearings is a stark contrast to dialogues in our own time that increasingly fall along strict party lines for topics far less disputable than agreeing the performance practice of the National Anthem. Indeed, a likely outcome of any current hearing would be an agreement that each side could pursue its own version, thus demonstrating independence and unity in collective division or, once again, hearings that do not lead to any further advancement in Congress. The consequence of this prolonged stasis has meant that, since Watergate (around which time Broyhill left Congress), the discussions, rather like Broyhill's many actions, have not been advanced. In the subsequent half-century, standardization has been replaced with increasing departures from the 'original' score. But, as we know from the Thomas Carr printing of 1814, embellishment was always part of the equation of performance practice. Whether embellishments heard by musicians, professional and amateur, in our own time can be seen as an extension of the original practice is a matter of interpretation and individual taste. By parallel, when the flag is discussed, numerous visual settings come to mind that reinforce a notion of patriotism, and yet, more recently, the image of the flag can be found on almost every item of clothing as well. If the National Anthem has followed a similar path of personal identification, then standardization meets an obstacle. One person's performance may offend another person, and *vice versa*, but we live in an age where a perceived or actual right toward individualism has overtaken what, to Ganz and other immigrants (especially from war-torn countries), would have been an essential unity in performance. To know that the National Anthem could be unchangeable provides solace to one person and a sense of unnecessary restriction to another. Putting aside questions of taste or individualism, I return to the question of the musical language and consider one topic that has been largely missed. When we consider the disagreements about modern performance practice, do we also rightfully consider a performance of Thomas Carr's version as viable? We are half a century on from the central advances of the Early Music Movement, and yet, performances of the National Anthem with stylistic embellishments of the period (ca. 1814) are rare. Indeed, by comparison, the versions of Damrosch and Sousa are remarkably conventional for their time compared to the ornamentation seen in Carr's version. If we are to consider the full range of options for performance practice, then the vigorous, brisk, approach once adopted becomes part of the discussion too. But where does that leave us? At a service of national mourning, this would be an inconceivable stylistic approach, and yet, a performance of the National Anthem would be wholly appropriate. Should this therefore mean that the National Anthem has potentially two basic approaches to performances, one lively and the other solemn. Once this debate begins, we return to the central question of standardization that surpasses rhythmic inequality between versions to see that no singular version could be democratically achieved in 1958, 1973, or indeed 2023. Thus, issues like rhythmic inequality are not only present but now historically legitimate insofar as they have become a common practice.

The debates around the National Anthem and the work of Rudolph Ganz in a culture of often nervous public patriotism reflect not just important historic discussions but a window into a time when such debates took place with a spirit of artistic and political engagement that was not driven by party affiliations or pronounced cultural individualism but by seeking to achieve unity through an ideal that is represented in the National Anthem.

Notes

1. Rudolph Ganz, *Naturalization*.
2. Colin H. Slim, "Stravinsky's Four Star-Spangled Banners and His 1941 Christmas Card," *The Musical Quarterly,* 89/2/3 (2006), 321–447.
3. Ibid., 322, 325.
4. Igor Stravinsky, *Banner.* Library of Congress ML 96.S44 Case, Vault.
5. Clague, *O Say Can You Hear?*, 234.
6. Ibid.
7. Leonard M. Libbey, "Yankee Blood Boils at Stravinsky's Act," *Boston Sunday Globe*, January 23, 1944, 17, Slim, "Stravinsky's Four Star-Spangled Banners and His 1941 Christmas Card," 414.
8. Ganz, "The Star-Spangled Banner," *Music Clubs*, April 1965, 19.
9. This comment aligns with Lichtenwanger's view on singing the high notes regardless of the vocal quality. Lichtenwanger, "Star-Spangled Banner. What Again?," 59–51.
10. "Arrest Karl Muck as an Enemy Alien," *The New York Times*, March 26, 1918, 3.
11. "The Star-Spangled Banner" Hearings, 50.
12. Henahan "Crimes Against Our Anthem".
13. John Philip Sousa, *National, Patriotic and Typical Airs of All Lands* (Philadelphia: Harry Coleman, 1890).
14. Ganz, "The Star-Spangled Banner," *Musical Facts*, April 1965, 19.
15. Hill, "A Proposed Official Version of the Star Spangled Banner," 40.
16. "The Star-Spangled Banner" Hearings, 74.
17. Hill died in 1961.
18. "The Star-Spangled Banner" Hearings, 70.
19. The moving bass line that annoyed Ganz in the National Anthem is also found in a similar fashion in the last stanza organ part for Hubert Parry's hymn tune to the words 'O Praise ye the Lord,' extracted from the larger anthem 'Hear my words, ye people'.
20. Ganz, "The Star-Spangled Banner" *Music Clubs*, April 1965, 19.
21. Letter from Sidney Yates to Rudolph Ganz, February 19, 1965.
22. Letter from Sidney Yates to Rudolph Ganz, February 1, 1967
23. Ferris, *Star-Spangled* Banner, 200. *Be Alert Bulletin*, U. S. Flag Committee. February 27, 1962.
24. Ferris, *Star-Spangled Banner*, 200–201.
25. Congressional Record – House, March 10, 2005. H1333.

Bibliography

Books and Articles

"An Original Idea," *Musical Courier*, 14 May, 1925.
"Arrest Karl Muck as an Enemy Alien," *The New York Times*, March 26, 1918.
Be Alert Bulletin, U. S. Flag Committee, January 10, 1958.
Amy Beegle, "American Music Education 1941–1946: Meeting Needs and Making Adjustments during World War II," *Journal of Historical Research in Music Education*, 26/1 (October, 2004).
Edmund Boles, "Karl Muck and His Compatriots: German Conductors in America during World War I (and How They Coped)," *American Music* 25 (2007).
E. Douglas Bomberger, "Taking the German Muse Out of Music: *The Chronicle* and US Musical Opinion in World War I," *Journal of the Society for American Music*, 14/2 (2020).
Joel T. Broyhill, "Statement Concerning House Joint Resolution 4," January 9, 1963.
Melissa D. Burrage, *The Karl Muck Scandal: Classical Music and Xenophobia in World War I America* (Rochester, NY: University of Rochester Press, 2019).
"Caruso Kisses Hand to America's Rocks," *New York World*, November 5, 1917.
Jeanne Colette Collester, *Rudolph Ganz – A Musical Pioneer* (Metuchen: The Scarecrow Press, 1995).
Mark Clague, *O Say Can You Hear?* (New York: W. W. Norton, 2022).
"Committee on American Unity Through Music, 'American Unity Through Music,'" *Music Educators Journal*, 27/5 (1941).
"Damrosch Too Against Anthem," *New York Evening Sun*, November 1, 1917.
Walter Damrosch, "One of the Noblest Functions," *Press and Sun-Bulletin* (Binghamton, NY), February 9, 1917.
Olin Downes, "Opera Opening," *The New York Times*, November 22, 1942.
Annegret Fauser, *Sounds of War: Music in the United States during World War II* (New York: Oxford University Press, 2013).
Robert H. Ferrell, *Grace Coolidge: The People's Lady in Silent Cal's White House* (Lawrence: University Press of Kansas, 2008), 81.
Marc Ferris, *Star-Spangled Banner* (Baltimore: Johns Hopkins University Press, 2014).
Four Principal National Songs (New York: American Book Company, 1912).
Rudolph Ganz, *Naturalization* (1925).
Rudolph Ganz, *The Whitehouse* (1929).
Rudolph Ganz, *Is There an American School of Composers* (late 1940s?).
Rudolph Ganz, *Music in the Threatened Areas* (1942).

Rudolph Ganz, "No War Propaganda – And a Great Conductor," *Musical Facts*, July–August, 1940.

Rudolph Ganz, "The Star-Spangled Banner," *Music Clubs*, April, 1965, 19.

"Ganz and Young St. Louis," *St. Louis Post Dispatch*, March 16, 1925.

Jessica C. E. Gienow-Hecht. *Sound Diplomacy: Music and Emotions in Transatlantic Relations, 1850–1920* (Chicago: University of Chicago Press, 2009).

William James Henderson, "Rising Tide of Sentiment Against German Music," *New York Sun*, December 2, 1917.

Donal J. Henahan "Crimes Against Our Anthem," *Chicago Daily News*, July 5, 1964.

Richard S. Hill, "A Proposed Official Version of the Star Spangled Banner," *Notes* 15, no. 1.

Charles Hopkins, "Rudolph Ganz," *Oxford Music Online* (accessed 1 March, 2023).

Alfred Human, "Ganz Breaks with German Composer," *Musical America*, 26 January, 1918 and 25 April, 1918.

Leonard M. Libbey, "Yankee Blood Boils at Stravinsky's Act," *Boston Sunday Globe*, January 23, 1944.

William Lichtenwanger, "Star-Spangled Bibliography," *College Music Symposium*, 12 (1972).

William Lichtenwanger, "Star-Spangled Banner. What Again?," *The Sonneck Society Newsletter*, 12/2 (Summer 1986).

Irving Lowens, "*L'affaire Muck*: A Study in War Hysteria (1917–1918)," *Musicology* 1 (1947).

Maj, H. L. "Higginson Defends Symphony," *Boston Globe*, November 1, 1917.

"Mr. Ganz Takes Leave of St. Louis Symphony," *The Christian Science Monitor*, 19 March, 1927.

Cleveland Moffett, "There Is Danger in German Music," *The Chronicle 4*, no. 1 (September, 1918.)

Matthew Mugmon, "Patriotism, Art, and 'The Star-Spangled Banner' in World War I: A New Look at the Karl Muck Episode," *Journal of Musicological Research*, 33 (2014).

NEA, *Journal of Proceedings and Addresses of the Forty-Seventh Annual Meeting Held in Denver, Colorado, July 309, 1909* (Winona, MN: The Association, 1909).

"Noted Singers Bring in $45,000 for Old 69th," *The New York Times*, September 23, 1918.

Bliss Perry, *The Life and Letters of Henry Lee Higginson* (Boston: The Atlantic Monthly Press, 1921.

Kevin Phillips, *The Cousins' Wars: Religion, Politics, and the Triumph of Anglo-America* (New York: Basic Books, 1999).

Elizabeth Pontiff, "MENC and the National Anthem; from the Early 1900s to Today's National Anthem," *Teaching Music*, 13/2 (October, 2005).

Eleanor Roosevelt, "Music Should Go On! A Message from the First Lady," *Musical America*, 62 (February 10, 1942).

Charles Seeger, "Wartime and Peacetime Programs in Music Education," *Music Educators Journal*, 29/3 (1943).

Colin Slim, "Stravinsky's Four Star-Spangled Banners and His 1941 Christmas Card," *The Musical Quarterly*, 89/(2–3) (2006), 321–447

Oscar George Sonneck and Library of Congress. Music Division. "The Star Spangled Banner" (Revised and Enlarged from the "Report" on the above and Other Airs, Issued in 1909) (Washington: Govt. print. off., 1914).

John Philip Sousa, *National, Patriotic and Typical Airs of All Lands* (Philadelphia: Harry Coleman, 1890).
John Chabot Smith, "Rudolph Ganz Cheered Wildly by Watergate Concert Crowd: 6,500 Cheer Ganz at Watergate Conductor Quiets Audience, After 2 Encores, by Playing National Anthem," *The Washington Post*, August 14, 1939.
Richard John Samuel Stevens, "Recollections," 1: 68, 70–73. Pendlebury Music. Library, Cambridge University.
John Philip Sousa, "What Our National Anthem Should Be: In Both Sentiment and Music, Says," *The New York Times*, August 26, 1928.
William Grant Still, "Composer Says 'Lend Lease' in Music Extends to Our Enemies," *Chicago Defender*, October 17, 1942.
Igor Stravinsky, *Banner*. Library of Congress ML 96.S44 Case, Vault.
Patrick Warfield, "Profitable Patriotism: John Philip Sousa and the Great War," *Over Here, Over There* (University of Illinois Press, 2019).

Correspondence

Letter from John Alden Carpenter to Carl Engel, November 4, 1918, Engel Papers, Music Division, Library of Congress, Washington, D.C.
Letter from Edwin Hughes National Music Council to Rudolph Ganz. November 17, 1964.
Letter from Edwin Hughes, National Music Council to Rudolph Ganz. January 13, 1965.
Letter from Arnold Gantvoort to Will Earhart, December 18, 1917, RG 12, NARA II.
Letter from Rudolph Ganz to Edwin Hughes. November 12, 1964.
Letter from Rudolph Ganz to Edwin Hughes. January 6, 1965.
Letter from Rudolph Ganz to Dr. Howard Hanson. June 15, 1964.
Letter to from Rudolph Ganz to Hans Walter Heinsheimer. July 26, 1964.
Letter to from Rudolph Ganz to Hans Walter Heinsheimer. July 28, 1964.
Letter from H. W. Heinsheimer, G. Schirmer, Inc. July 28, 1964.
Letter from Howard Hanson to Rudolph Ganz, Eastman School of Music. August 3, 1964.
Letter from Helen Lasell to George Radcliff, President, Maryland Historical Society, undated, typewritten letter. Cited manuscripts in Maryland Historical Society.
Letter from Elsie M. Shawe to Theodore Roosevelt, October 28, 1907, Record Group 12, Entry 6, Historical Files, File Class 900, Box 68, National Archives and Records Administration, College Park, MD. (RG 12, NARA II).
Letter from Harold Spivacke, Chief, Music Division, The Library of Congress to Rudolph Ganz, July 27, 1964.
Letter from Sidney Yates to Rudolph Ganz, February 19, 1965.
Letter from Sidney Yates to Rudolph Ganz, February 1, 1967.

Congressional Records

Congressional Record – House, March 10, 2005. H1333.
"The Star-Spangled Banner" Hearings before Subcommittee No. 4 of the Committee on the Judiciary, House of Representatives, May 21, 22, and 28, 1958 (Washington: US Government Printing Office).

Index

American Composers Alliance 24
American Federation of Musicians
   (Local 802) 24
American Legion (Department of
   Maryland) 60
Anacreontic Society 36–37, 38

Barlow, S. 24
Beegle, A. 22
Begich, N. 79
Boggs, H. 79–80
Bomberger, D. E. 2, 6–7, 17, 24
Boulanger, (N. or L?) 30
Boulanger, N. 32
Britten, B. 30, 32
Broyhill, J. T. 46–50, 53–54, 62, 66–69,
   72–74, 76, 79–81
Burkhardt, D. H. 60–61
Bush, L. 80

Carpenter, J. A. 8, 43
Carr, T. 37, 39, 40, 47, 75, 81–82
Caruso, E. 58
Castelnuovo-Tedesco, M. 30
Clague, M. 2, 37, 43, 44, 67
Cliburn, V. 68–69
Clinton, W. J. 80
*The Code for the National Anthem of the
   United States of America* 39, 44
Coolidge, C. 9, 11, 36
Coolidge, G. 10
Copland, A. 9, 24

Damrosch, W. 6, 18, 24, 42, 43–44, 58,
   67–70, 72–75, 82
Debussy, C. 17, 19, 21
Dorn, F. E. 53–54, 69
Downes, O. 21
Drabkin, M. 49, 61
Dykema, P. W. 42, 45

Earhart, W. 43
Eisenhower, D. D. 68, 76, 79

Farrar, G. 8
Fauser, A. 2, 9, 24
Ferris, M. 2
Fithian, P. G. 42
Forrester, E. L. 49–50, 53–54

Gantvoort, A. 42–43
Ganz, R.: *Music in the Threatened
   Areas* 21, 26–27, 45;
   Naturalization 13–14, 23, 33;
   *No War Propaganda–And a
   Great Conductor* 18, 33; *The
   Whitehouse* 9–11
Gienow-Hecht, J. C. E. 6, 28–29
Griffes, C. 5
Griffin, A. P. C. 42

Hanson, H. 2, 3, 8–9, 46, 69–70,
   73–75
Heinsheimer, H. W. 69–70, 72
Henderson, W. J. 8
Henahan, D. J. 47, 67, 69–70
Herbert, V. 18, 20, 42, 68, 70
Higginson, H. L. 18–20, 38
Hijman, J. 30
Hill, R. S. 2, 36–37, 46–48, 50, 52, 55,
   61, 62, 72, 76
Hindemith, P. 30, 32
Hoar, E. R. 38
Hofmann, J. 66, 68, 69, 75
Holland, E. J. 49, 61
Hoover, H. 46, 53
Horowitz, V. 66
Hughes, E. 69, 73–75
Humperdinck, E. 6
Hunt, H. 79

Independent Citizens Committee for the
   Arts, Sciences, and Professions
   in New York 24

Johnson, H. 24
Johnson, T. 8–9

Key, F. S. 37, 43, 46–47, 53, 68
Key, P. 15
Kindler, H. 69
Korngold, E. 5, 30
Kreisler, F. 8
Krenek, E. 30

Lasell, H. P. 48, 50, 79
Libbey, L. M. 67
Lichtenwanger, W. 2, 38, 58
Liddy, G. G. 79
Linthicum, J. C. 45

MacDowell, E. 29
Mason, W. 29
McBride, W. B. 46
McCormack, J. 8, 47, 68
Moffett, C. 7
Monroe, J. 58
Monroe, L. 48, 55, 58
Muck, K. 6, 7, 11, 16, 21, 23, 32, 33, 36, 44, 68, 70
Mugmon, M. 17, 44
Music Educators National Conference (MENC) 22, 45
Music Supervisors' National Conference (MSNC) 42, 43, 45
Music Teachers National Association (MTNA) 22

National Association of Schools of Music (NASM) 9
National Education Association (NEA) 42–43, 80
National Music Council (NMC) 46, 50, 51, 54, 68, 72–75
Nichol, C. B. 49, 61
Nimtz, F. J. 62
Nixon, R. M. 79

O'Neill, T. P. 80

Paderewski, I. 14
Poe, T. 80
Pontiff, E. 45

Putnam, H. 42

Rachmaninoff, S. 66
Roosevelt, E. 24–25
Roosevelt, T. 1, 2, 39, 44, 66, 76

St. Louis Symphony Orchestra 5, 12–17, 23, 29, 44
Schoenberg, A. 30, 31–32
Seeger, C. 23
Shawe, E. 2, 39, 44, 76
Sherwood, W. 29
Slim, C. H. 66
Smith, A. T. 47, 67
Smith, J. S. 36–37, 46
Sonneck, O. G. 2, 42, 43
Sousa, J. P. 30, 42–45, 58, 67, 70, 72, 82
Spivacke, H. 72
Spofford, A. R. 42
Stevens, R. J. S. 37
Stravinsky, I. 65–66, 67–68
Still, W. G. 27
Stock, F. 68–69
Swiss American Historical Society 16

Taubman, P. 48, 50, 56–61, 71
Taylor, D. 30, 55, 59, 72
Teta, A. R. 46
Toch, E. 30

United Service Organizations (USO) 24
U. S. Flag Committee 48

Warfield, P. 2, 44
Weinberger, J. 30
The White House 9–13, 36, 65
Whitener, B. L. 49, 52–53, 55, 68
Witherspoon, B. 24
Works Progress Administration (WPA) (New York) 24

Yates, S. R. 75

Zelenko, H. 49, 54–55, 58, 61

For Product Safety Concerns and Information please contact our EU
representative GPSR@taylorandfrancis.com
Taylor & Francis Verlag GmbH, Kaufingerstraße 24, 80331 München, Germany

www.ingramcontent.com/pod-product-compliance
Lightning Source LLC
Chambersburg PA
CBHW051758230426
43670CB00012B/2337